HELLENISTIC ARCHITECTURE IN ASIA MINOR

Representation of Prometheus, in the museum at Side

HELLENISTIC
ARCHITECTURE
IN ASIA MINOR

JAMES STEELE
PHOTOGRAPHS BY ERSIN ALOK

OPPOSITE: *Hellenistic watchtowers at the main gates of Perge;*
ABOVE: *Coffered decorations showing tragic and comic masks, Didyma*

ACKNOWLEDGEMENTS

This book would not have been possible without the foresight of my publisher, Andreas Papadakis, whom I sincerely thank for his support and patience. I also acknowledge the assistance of Demetri Porphyrios and Richard Economakis, in advising me on its contents. Dean Wayne Drummond provided me with much needed support during the course of the writing and made it possible for Ann Knudsen to contribute all of the drawings used throughout. I would also like to thank the design and editorial team at Academy Editions, namely Andrea Bettella, Vivian Constantinopoulos, Helen Castle, Nicola Hodges and Jan Richter.   *James Steele*

COVER: The Temple of Athena, Priene

First published in Great Britain in 1992 by
ACADEMY EDITIONS
An imprint of the Academy Group Ltd, 42 Leinster Gardens London W2 3AN
ISBN: 0 85670 981 6

Published in the United States by
ST MARTIN'S PRESS, 175 FIFTH AVENUE, NEW YORK, NY 10010
ISBN: 0-312-08112-X

Printed and bound in Singapore

CONTENTS

INTRODUCTION

The Hellenistic Age, which started with Alexander's consolidation of power after the death of Philip, and ended at Actium, has frequently been characterised as having begun as an idealistic crusade. Yet that was only one of the motivating factors behind it. Driven by the wish to emulate the deeds of the heroes in his beloved *Iliad*, and the complex desire both to exact recompense for past atrocities committed against a cultural heritage he wanted to assimilate and to disseminate those values throughout the East, Alexander's initial intentions seem at first to have been framed by the need for vengeance, as well as fame. His frequently misunderstood accommodation of the cultures he sought to transform, as well as the imitative syncretism that it fostered in many of his followers, is one of the most underrated achievements of this age, and the combination of influences that is evident in the architecture that has survived in Asia Minor, is its most legible legacy. The exposure to and acceptance of other cultures, which he actively encouraged has consistently been listed as the primary cause behind the degeneration of the classical canon, but the examples shown here lend credence to the argument that such opinions must be more carefully qualified.

In one of the most balanced assessments that has yet to appear concerning the intellectual cross-fertilisation that took place during the transition from the Classical to the Hellenistic period, Christine Mitchell Havelock has cited the temple form as the clearest example of symbiosis between East and West. In addition, she has compared Alexander's invasion of Asia Minor with the earlier, Doric conquest of the Greek mainland in terms of the effect that it had upon existing architecture, saying that,

> it should come as no surprise that many of the dramatic changes that occurred in the design of the Ionic Temple in the period after Alexander have their source in Attica . . . Just as it was impossible for the mainland architects of the fifth century to abandon their Doric heritage when they adopted Ionic elements, so it was impossible for architects working in Asia Minor during the Hellenistic Age to forego entirely their own traditions.

And yet, as she specifies,

> an underlying order, based upon numerical proportions, instilled rationality into the arrangement of elements. No one temple exhibited all these features, but each of them, (such) as the temples at Sardis, Magnesia, Didyma and others . . . included more than one. The clear structure of the parts and the overall unity and coherence compel us to see these temples as 'classical' examples of the Ionic order. This architectural style we may justifiably call 'Ionic-Attic'.[1]

The growing awareness of individuality, of a personality separate from the *polis*, that begins to become evident in the Hellenistic Age, was necessitated by exponential turmoil resulting from constant warfare, and a concomitant loss of democracy in long established city states. In pejorative, dismissive terms, Nikos Kazantzakis has characterised the objectivity that this engendered as degenerative, by saying that:

> In Greece, as everywhere, once realism begins to reign, civilisation declines. Thus we arrive at the realistic, magniloquent and faithless Hellenistic era, which was devoid of supra-personal ideals. From chaos to the Parthenon, then from the Parthenon back to chaos, the great merciless rhythm. Emotions and passions run wild. The free individual loses his powers of discipline; the bridle which maintained instinct in strict balance flies from his hands. Passion, emotionality, realism . . . A mystical, melancholy yearning suffuses the faces. The fearful mythological visions become merely decorative . . . After the Peloponnesian war Greece begins to disintegrate. Belief in the fatherland is lost; individual self-sufficiency triumphs.[2]

In that self-sufficiency, however, we can recognise contemporary parallels which now elude us in a loftier, Classical Age, as well as a tantalising modern spatial vision similarly qualified by a single station point and progression into, rather than around a work of architecture. While many historians often look to the Renaissance as the critical point of this change in perception, Pergamon and Didyma stand as compelling evidence of an earlier transition from social to individual awareness.

The process of syncretism which, more specifically, may be said to have begun with the first, early colonies that were established on the Aegean coast of Asia Minor, and to have been spread by Alexander's methodical conquest of even the most remote indigenous cities in Lycia, Cilicia and the interior, was incremental, affecting each area differently. Ironically, it was those who were Hellenised last who seemed most vigorously to promote the ideals introduced by Alexander, in yet another instance of proselytes outdistancing their teacher. In these cities, which are primarily located inland from the Mediterranean coast, the commonly recurring institutions of temple, theatre, gymnasium and bouleuterion are integral to overall urban form. The cities in Lycia, in particular, which was one of the last of the regions to feel Greek influence, most clearly represent this remarkable dichotomy by illustrating ideological synthesis, on the one hand, and a complete retention of their individuality on the other. In sharp contrast to the cerebral, orthogonal logic of Miletus, which is the definitive example of Hippodamian planning, or other interpretations, adapting to far more difficult topographical conditions at Priene and Herakleia, these Lycian cities have a natural, elemental quality, directly related to their particular sites. While the gridiron of Priene, with its central cluster of public buildings stretched out as a spine through the middle of the city, works in spite of, rather than because of, its steep, cliffside location, Lycian centres such as Xanthos, Termessos, Labranda and Arycanda all seem to be perfect extensions of their *genius loci*.

The series of events that began with the bequest of Pergamon and its dependencies by Attalus III and continued on with the assimilation of Kommagene into the Province of Syria in 72 AD, increasingly embroiled an initially reluctant Rome deeper and deeper into Asia Minor. In the process, the Romans found the evolving Hellenistic preference for sensationalism and sophisticated and impressive internal spaces, to be especially suited to the needs of their growing Empire. The points of similarity as well as the differences between Hellenistic and Roman architecture are very instructive of the essential nature of the change that took place after Alexander, and are most clearly read in the temple. The process of evolution, from the Parthenon to the temple of Didyma of 300 BC and finally in the Temple of Zeus at Aizanoi, which was built during the reign of Hadrian, between 117 and 130 AD, is very clear, presenting tangible evidence of profound change. If, to quote Kazantzakis again, the Parthenon is 'a feat of the intellect – of numbers, geometry, a faultless thought enmarbled, a sublime achievement of the mind, possessing every virtue',[3] it fails to touch the human soul as Didyma and Aizanoi both do. While the Parthenon is three dimensional, sculptural, plastic and serene in its exalted position on the Acropolis, the temple of Apollo at Didyma is longitudinal and axial, with a singular emphasis on the chresmographeion which is also the single entrance at its eastern end. Although it was built in the Roman period, Aizanoi follows the rules set down by the Hellenistic architect Hermogenes, with a pseudo diptertal arrangement of columns and peristasis surrounding its naos which are typical of attempts by builders working during the reign of one of the first emperors to pattern himself after the Macedonian philosopher-king, to establish links with the past. As Ekrem Akurgal has said, 'one is struck by the neo-classical character of the art forms of the Hadrianic period, as manifest in the rendering of the architectural ornamentation, the egg and dart mouldings, the composite capitals and especially the acanthus leaves on the middle akroterion.'[4] The duality that becomes obvious here is that in addition to the evolution from classical containment through Hellenistic extroversion and Roman aggrandisation of scale that these three temples represent, there was an equal and opposite emulation of classical elements in Asia Minor that began during Hadrian's reign which makes synchronic analysis difficult. All that can be said with any assurance is, that with the exception of theatre construction which brought Latin engineering instincts to the same high pitch that the design of fortifications had engendered among the Successors, the tectonic genealogy between Hellenistic and Roman architecture is very strong in Asia Minor springing as it does from comparable world views. The layering of the two is so entwined in many of the sites there that it is difficult to identify a pure Hellenistic city, while identification of principles and the subsequent expression of the ideals promoted by Alexander is clear.

In order to place this entire period in its proper historical perspective and correct geographical context, it should be remembered that at the time the Hellenistic cities in Asia Minor were in their ascendancy, Athens was in serious decline. From its former position at the head of the Delian League in 477 BC, which Pericles had skilfully used as a patriotic pretext for making his city the centre of an empire, Athens had benefitted, both economically and culturally, from its far flung dependencies. The participation of each of the colonies across the Aegean was an especially important part of this initiative, since the Athenians claimed Ionian heritage and the perpetuation of this culture, as Havelock has noted, 'had a political motive since it allowed Athens (as) a city on the predominantly Doric mainland, to hold up the imperialist banner of pan-Hellenism'.[5]

Following the Peloponnesian war with Sparta this predominance was ended and Athens was politically, spiritually and financially bankrupt. While the focus of power had unquestionably shifted to Macedon, and severe economic and social conditions supplied a second, more pragmatic agenda for an idealistic crusade to the East, the city remained a symbol of the aspirations of all who wanted to identify themselves with what it had represented in the past. Havelock has put it more succinctly when she has said that: 'To Alexander and all his successors, Greek culture meant primarily Athenian culture with all its desired pan-Hellenic overtones'.⁶ The iconographic importance that it had is further substantiated by the architectural contributions that various Hellenistic kings made to it, such as the recently restored stoa of Attalus II, and the middle stoa of Ptolemy VI. Such contributions to a distant city represent an unparalleled sense of duty, only approximated by the various dynastic additions to the Temple of Amon at Karnak, with a spiritual equivalent being the *hieromenia*, or 'sacred month' of the games, when friends and enemies from the most extreme reaches of Hellenic influence would forget their differences and converge on Olympia to compete with one another. Athens, which had been an implacable task master in the past, became the beneficiary of the respect of its foes, with the evidence of that respect being most obvious today.

Other monuments such as the Tower of the Winds, which was built in 40 BC and is recorded as having been designed by an astronomer named Andronikos from Kyrrhos in Syria, confirm the extent of eastern Hellenic ideas, as well as patronage, in Athens at this time. Standing as it does near the Agora, which has traditionally represented the fulcrum of Greek culture, it is indicative of a growing awareness of distant horizons that is characteristic of its age, and the relative value of time, which was counted out by both a sundial and clepsederia inside the tower. It is one of the most imaginative non-sacred structures of the time, and the most indicative of the intellectual cross-references then at work.

As a final irony, the name Macedonia has now taken on the same symbolic aspects that Athens had in the Hellenistic period, raising similar passions and hopes, both among Greeks and neighbouring Slavic people to the North, aware of the historical and cultural legacy associated with the region. History now seems to have come full circle and the emotions that this name evokes show that Alexander's desire to assume the mantle of pan-Hellenism has succeeded beyond his wildest dreams.

ABOVE: Winged griffin, Didyma; p 6: The Temple of Zeus, Aizanoi

Map of Asia Minor

Lycian sarcophagus discovered in the royal necropolis at Sidon, along with the so-called 'Alexander Sarcophagus', detail

ALEXANDER

Achilles, whom Zeus loved, now rose. Around his shoulders Athena hung her shield, like a thunderhead with trailing fringe.
Goddess of goddesses bound his head with a golden cloud, and made his very body blaze with fiery light.
Homer, 'The Immortal Shield', Book 18, *The Iliad.*[1]

While much has been written about the unparalleled achievements of Alexander the Great, little or none of it even begins to reveal the real personality of the man himself, or the influences behind the ideas that drove him. While much of this vagueness may understandably be attributed to the abstractions of time, or the politically motivated inaccuracies in contemporary sources, or even the nationalistic or academic encumbrances of the present, the facts that do exist now seem to allow for a more personal view of this remarkable man. While it is, of course, impossible ever really to know the true purpose of the young general who led his army across what must have seemed like the endless expanse of the Granicus River and into the midst of the Persian army massed on its eastern shore, there can be no argument about the fact that the consequence of that single act was the beginning of the Hellenistic Age.

Using a fractious Greek and Macedonian force to invade an enormously large kingdom, which was then held by a numerically superior army with an extremely efficient system of supply may now seem precipitous and brash, but it was an event that Alexander had prepared for all of his life.

His father, Philip, who was the first of the three main influences in Alexander's life, had become King of Macedon in 359 BC, and had claimed descent from the man/god Herakles through his father, Amynthas III, and the Argead dynasty from the Peloponnese. This dynasty, which had ruled Macedon for four hundred years before Philip had taken the throne, had never succeeded in totally uniting the Greek mainland, and Philip, upon his kingship, persistently set out to consolidate the many isolated city-states around him. Beginning with Amphipolis on his eastern border, and continuing on with the capture of Polidaea, Pudna, Thessaly, Epirus and Olythus in their turn, Philip continued his expansion until Athens became alarmed at his growing strength. While struggling along in a war of their own against Euboea nearby, the Athenians, and more particularly Demosthenes, who was so convincing in his oratory against the Macedonean push, called out for an alliance against what they perceived to be a new threat to their own quest for power. As Robin Lane Fox, who has written so much on Alexander, has said: 'In Philip we meet the greatest builder of a kingdom and army in the ancient world.'[2] His success in building that kingdom seemed to have as much to do with luck and historical circumstance as it did with strategic skill and persistence, and he was unarguably to pass his proclivity for each on to his son Alexander. The growing Greek alliance against Philip, led by Athens, continued to gather strength and finally combined to face him at Chaeronia, to the east in Delphi, in 338 BC. The eighteen-year-old Alexander fought with his father in this decisive battle, which has long been remembered for the valour displayed on each side, and has been commemorated by the large statue of a lion that still stands on the site. With this victory, and the peace of the League of Corinth that followed soon afterwards, Philip had finally achieved what he had originally set out to do. As the final victor in this long series of struggles for leadership of the Hellenic world, he was the logical choice for the focus of all of Isocrates' hopes, who called for a Greek crusade against the Persian 'barbarians' in 346 BC. This appeal, which was very similar in fervour to that raised by the church against the 'infidels' who occupied the Holy Land in the Middle Ages, called on Philip to build an army, because of his proven ability to unite what had previously been a series of hopelessly fragmented Hellenic city-states. In his appeal, Isocrates also made frequent reference to Philip's Argead legitimacy, and the fact that because his ancestor Herakles had laid waste to The Troad in the past, it was all the more fitting that Philip should do the same once more.[3] Alexander was ten years old when Isocrates made the first call for his father to lead a crusade into Asia; and the inevitable discussion at court and the ensuing preparations that were the main focus of attention for the next decade surely made an indelible impression upon a young man of such an impressionable age. Philip, however, was assassinated in July of 336 BC, before his final plans for the invasion could be implemented. He had, however, already sent a sizeable reconnaissance mission into Persian-occupied Phrygia, and this mission had produced an extraordinary peace offering from a Carian satrap named Pixodarus in anticipation of the imminent Greek invasion of, and probable victory over, the whole area.

In crossing the Granicus, then, Alexander was not impulsively beginning another war with an ancient and hated enemy that had proven implacable in the past, but was instead acting to fulfil his father's abortive intention to carry out the crusade called for by Isocrates, and finally made official by the Council of Corinth in 336.

In addition to inheriting Philip's mandate for the liberation of all of the Persian held cities in Asia Minor, as well as most of his father's luck, sense of opportunity and quick grasp of strategy, Alexander was also blessed with the same physical toughness that had enabled Philip to see personally to the execution of all of the decisions that he made. Of the few portrait studies done at the time, those on a funerary cot recently excavated in Vergina, which was once the Macedonian royal city of Aigai, tell much about the characters of Philip, his wife Olympias and their son Alexander.[4] The portrait of Philip that has been retrieved from this particular cot, clearly reveals a middle-aged man in a close-cropped beard, who has the face and nose of a fighter. The deeply-etched furrows on his brow, however, are those brought on by the responsibilities that his ambitions have imposed upon him and are also unmistakably present. In spite of having one sightless eye, which is known to have been blinded in battle, Philip has an unnervingly steadfast look; and this, along with his slightly annoyed impatient expression, give the overall impression of a man whom it would not be pleasant to have as an enemy. Beyond the obvious toughness, however, there is a revealing soft side to him, exposed by the full lines of a mouth just visible through his beard. This added depth indicates a more gentle and far less martial character. Although his personal history clearly outlines the record of a battle-scarred and case-hardened soldier, there is also the occasional hint of another, more emotional dimension to him that is perhaps attributable to his Illyrian mother, Eurydice, and it is this emotional side that may explain his initial attraction to his wife, Alexander's mother, Olympias.

The first encounter between Philip and Olympias is thought to have been during a performance of the mysteries at the Sanctuary of the Gods on the island of Samothrace in 357 BC.[5] The young princess, who was by then orphaned, was the daughter of King Neoptolemus of the Molassian tribe of Epirus, who in turn traced his descent directly from the Homeric hero Achilles. Her Epirean birthplace is also thought to have been the etymological origin of the term 'Hellas', itself because of the Hellopes tribe in that area, who traditionally supplied the priests for the temple of Dordona that was in the same region.[6] These deep-rooted ethnic credentials, combined with a recurring tendency towards high-mindedness, may explain why the princess, who had first been named Polyxene, had later decided to change her given name to one that she felt would honour the ideas of the athletes who completed for glory at the base of Mount Olympus, and thus give her some identification with them.

On both his paternal and maternal sides then, Alexander could and did lay claim to cultural roots that mixed ancient myths of gods and heroes with hereditary reality in a way that would have been saturated with double meanings in that age. The same degree of idealistic fervour that had originally prompted Olympias to change her name, as well as to travel to distant places to take part in religious mysteries and to become increasingly preoccupied with the Homeric strains in her family background, also eventually led to a deep mysticism that began to border on hysteria. While existing portraiture of Philip conveys a man who is impatient and has a great deal on his mind, his level gaze unquestionably indicates that his mind is sound. With Olympias, however, there is the heavy lidded, intense and wide-eyed stare of a medium who is both very much of this world, and yet quite separate from it. Her unflinchingly penetrating eyes, combined with an elongated, aquiline nose and perpetually pursed lips, seem to confirm the possibility of all of the excesses that have been attributed to her, such as her legendary zeal in making religious sacrifices.[7] The extent of this mysticism and its full influence upon Alexander, while difficult to trace, were undoubtedly contributing factors behind several of his most uncharacteristically melodramatic actions, such as his mysterious expedition to the shrine of Zeus Amon at the Siwah Oasis, and the bacchanal that led to the burning of the palaces of Persepolis, several years later.

When Alexander was thirteen, Philip, with foresight, decided to send him away from the many distractions of the court at Pella to the quiet country town of Mieza, for advanced studies. In one of the most delightful coincidences of history, Philip also chose the philosopher Aristotle of Stageira, in Chalcidice, to direct those studies as Alexander's tutor. In assuming this role, Aristotle became the third key influence in the life of the young prince, and this influence can be clearly seen in all of the later historical descriptions of the king's boundless intellectual curiosity, his love of literature, poetry and drama and his patronage of artists and political and civic development. Where Olympias may have passed on some degree of her Dionysian mysticism to him, Aristotle countered it with his Apollonian detachment and objectivity, giving Alexander the intellectual depth to deal with his heightened gift of vision. As WW Tarn has said: 'So far as his character was influenced by others, it was influenced by Aristotle and Olympias, by a philosopher who taught that moderation alone could hold a kingdom together and by a woman to whom any sort of moderation was unknown.'[8] While that particular lesson may have slipped Alexander's mind occasionally, and most certainly passed over the heads of his successors, the sheer joy of intellectual pursuit did not, and his encouragement of the arts left an indelible stamp upon the Hellenistic Age that followed. At the time of his appointment, Aristotle was about forty years old, and had not yet reached the apex of his fame. He had just come from the coastal city of Assos in Asia Minor, after having set up a school of philosophy there. As a former pupil of Plato himself, and one of the founders of the Lyceum in Athens, Aristotle was certainly in full command of all of the branches of knowledge at that time, and had greatly contributed to the full extent of each of them. He is most well known for his brilliant criticisms of Plato, as well as his highly individualised system of logic, and is credited with single-handedly evolving the new science of biology.

The full scope of the concepts that he passed on to Alexander is not specifically known, but much can be inferred from his concurrent writings, as well as from statements and directives issued by Alexander later on in his campaigns. In addition to highly probable studies of Homer's *Iliad* and *Odyssey*, several other important works, that have since been lost, were known to have been written by Aristotle specifically for these tutorials. Their existence is further confirmed through references to them by historians like Cicero, as well as in a letter written by Alexander himself, in which he protested that Aristotle had made public the lectures that were supposedly written only for him.[9] Additional references also reveal that one of these works may have been based on Plato's ideal of a philosopher-king who would govern his subjects in an enlightened way, while a second, which was entitled *To Alexander*, or *On the Colonists*, stressed the importance of both maintaining existing colonies in Asia Minor and establishing new ones.[10] Each of these were obviously delivered with great effect, probably in the peripatetic way then in fashion in Athens which would allow a single teacher to retain the attention of a group of young men.

While it is tempting to conjure up a vision of one of the best philosophers that the world has ever known having prolonged and private discussions with the future conqueror of the ancient world, it is believed that there were almost certainly other students in the sacred grove at Mieza. These possibly included Alexander's closest friends Hephaestion, Nearchus, and Craterus.

Such teaching, when layered upon the knowledge of his father's sense of mission and his mother's tales of heroic ancestral deeds and supernatural conception, give his unprecedented invasion a degree of inevitability that Tarn has quite eloquently described as his 'inheritance'.[11] According to Macedonian tradition, however, Philip's throne itself was not an automatic part of that inheritance, and had to be rewon by force. Alexander's first acts as king, after Philip's assassination, were threefold. He moved rapidly to eliminate any other possible heirs, to re-establish his leadership of the League of Corinth and his own mandate to attack the 'barbarians' in Asia Minor, and to recall the veteran general Parmenion, who had been sent there by his father at the head of a reconnaissance mission. Only when his own authority was firmly established did he set out, and while his army was sizeable, it consisted of far more than just fighting men, taking on the complexion of an expedition rather than just a military campaign, similar to that of Napoleon's occupation of Egypt. In addition to the physicians, technicians, historians, philosophers and biologists that were included in it, there were a group of surveyors, called Bematists, who compiled topographical data about the physical characteristics of the route that the army took, and these surveys made up the only geographic information about the East for centuries to follow.

After his exhilarating victory of the Granicus, Alexander's first official public act in Asia Minor was to make a pilgrimage to the barren, windswept plain of Ilion in order to pay homage to the ideals embodied in the long struggle that Homer had so forcefully described, and to show his respect for

Achilles, with whom he identified so closely. In a dramatic, perceptive and unmistakably imitative act of homage, Alexander stripped off his armour and ran a great distance to the tomb of his ancestor, to place a garland upon it. This single act recalled, in a graphically physical way, the vivid image of the heartless, superhumanly strong warrior who had run the Trojan champion Hector to the ground. As Homer has so chillingly described this scene:

Now close at hand
Achilles like the implacable god of war
came on with blowing crest hefting the dreaded
beam of Pelian ash for his right shoulder.
Bronze light played around him, like the glare
of a great fire or the great sun rising,
and Hector, as he watched, began to tremble.
Then he could hold his ground no more. He ran
leaving the gate behind him, with Achilles hard
on his heels, sure of his own speed.
When that most lightning-like of birds, a hawk
bred on a mountain, swoops upon a dove,
the quarry dips in terror, but the hunter,
screaming, dips behind and gains upon it,
passionate for prey. Just so Achilles
murderously left the air, as Hector
ran with flashing knees along the wall.[12]

Following this most personal gesture of both emotional and genetic kinship, Alexander claimed the great shield of Achilles that still remained at the tomb; in full recognition of its symbolic value as both tangible evidence of his own link with the Homeric hero, and of the continuity of the Hellenic determination to right the wrongs committed against them by those occupying Trojan soil. He was also, of course, aware of Homer's description of the creation of this shield in *The Iliad*, by Hephaestus, the god of fire, at the request of Achilles' mother Thetis.

In crucibles the twenty bellows breathed
every degree of fiery air: to serve him . . .
durable fine bronze and tin he threw into the blaze
with silver and with honourable gold,
then mounted a big anvil in his block
and in his right hand took a powerful hammer,
managing with his tongs in his left hand.
His first job was a shield, a broad one, thick,
well-fashioned everywhere. A shining rim
he gave it, triple-ply, and hung from this
a silver shoulder strap. Five welded layers
composed the body of the shield. The maker

used all his art adorning this expanse.

He pictured on it earth, heaven, and sea,

unwearied sun, moon waxing, all the stars

that heaven bears for garland: Pleiades,

Hyades, Orion in his might,

the Great Bear, too, that some have called the Wain,

pivoting there, attentive to Orion and unbathed

ever in the Ocean stream.[13]

After this description of the zodiac, Homer goes into a lengthy dialogue about other scenes shown on the shield, such as contrasting views of a city at peace and a city at war, rural harvests, grape-filled vineyards, the bloody killing of a bull by lions, and a dance in which young boys and girls 'circled in ease'. In conclusion, he writes:

Then, running round the shield-rim, triple-ply, he

pictured all the might of the Ocean stream.

Besides the densely plated shield, he made

a cuirass, brighter far than fire light,

a massive helmet, measured for his temples,

handsomely figured, with a crest of gold;

then greaves of pliant tin.

Now when the crippled god

had done his work, he picked up all the arms

and laid then down before Achilles' mother.[14]

Much effort has historically been spent in interpreting the possible allegory in this famous passage. The predominant consensus is that Hephaestus himself represented the all–engulfing fire that created the shapeless universe, and that the circular shield represents the cosmos, or the bringing of order out of chaos. The bronze and tin and silver and gold used in the construction were taken to represent the four elements, and its three layers, the earth, sky and sea, surrounded by the heavenly bodies. The five zones into which the shield is divided may also stand for the five circles of heaven.[15]

In a deeper sense then, such allegorical interpretation must have also influenced Alexander's wish to possess the shield, which was similar to a Hellenic holy grail. Having this magical symbol of the cosmos made him a king with powers that surpassed human frailty; and transformed him into a cosmocrator, the ruler of the universe.[16]

The Iliad itself, is a classic example of Aristotle's dictum of the efficiency of economy of time, place and action in epic poetry. It revolves around the story of the death of the Trojan hero Hector, and focuses on one brief period in the ten year siege of the city. In that time the hopes and ambitions of two armies are concentrated into a single combat between Achilles and Hector, who were selected as the champions of each side. In this desperate struggle, which is one of the key events in the entire story, the dichotomy between the two combatants is sharply drawn. Hector, as the champion of Troy, is depicted as a dutiful husband and son who is both fully aware of, and comfortable with his responsibilities to his family and his city. Achilles, on the other hand, always seems to be aloof from social obligations of this sort, fighting in a dispassionate, implacable way to revenge the death of his friend Patroclos, and not specifically for the Achaean cause. His is a personal, not a social agenda, guided by arcane and ultimately selfish motives. While never actually accused of arrogance by Homer in the poem itself, he was often depicted as such in the popular art of the time, showing that the full implications of his actions were clearly understood within the value system of his own culture.

In spite of, or perhaps because of this extreme individuality, Achilles remains the most clearly drawn and unforgettable of all of the heroic characters described in *The Iliad*. He is the ultimate warrior, totally devoid of human compassion, whose mechanical detachment evokes an almost perverse admiration, and whose lack of normal social instincts give him the ability to see things more objectively than others. This detachment, in turn, projects a divine aura around him, that contravenes the normal Greek attitude about the void that separates gods and men.

By choosing Achilles as a paradigm, Alexander himself began to personify and popularise singular rather than communal concerns, and by doing so, helped to crystalise the subliminal Hellenic belief in the basic worth and importance of the individual. His awakening of the idea of the divine spark in each human being, that had always lurked just beneath the surface in Greek culture, eventually began to threaten the communal unity that was so implicitly vital to the social contract of the polis, and the cohesiveness that had separated the Greeks so emphatically from other civilisations, such as those of Egypt and Sumer.

Initially lacking a Patroclos of his own to avenge, Alexander instead adopted the cause of Greek honour, which had been disgraced by the Persian 'barbarians' in the past. Using this cause as a rallying cry, he stated that the eventual freedom of all of the Hellenic peoples under their domination was his ultimate goal. Darius, the Great King, thus became his Hector, the one whom he sought personally to slay and drag through the dust behind him in fulfilment of what he interpreted to be his Homeric legacy. This opponent, however, was to prove more elusive than he had expected, and did not fight by Homeric rules. Alexander was consequently forced to manoeuvre him into one encounter after another, and was drawn deeper and deeper into Asia in the process. Nearly a thousand years after the epic struggle between Achilles and Hector had taken place on the plains of Ilion, Alexander found himself pursuing his reluctant quarry from the Granicus to Issus and finally across the Tigris River itself, perpetually seeking the decisive person-to-person confrontation that he had always hoped for, without ever finding it. A famous Roman mosaic now on display in the House of the Faun in Pompeii, that had been copied from an original Greek painting done soon after the battle of Issus in 333 BC, graphically shows a critical moment in that struggle. In it a wild-eyed Darius, in the midst of his disintegrating army, is surrounded by a forest of Macedonian Sarissas, and frantically looks directly into the eyes of the fair-haired nemesis trying desperately to fight his way through the mêlée to get to the Persian King.

This is the closest that Alexander ever got to his much sought after moment of personal revenge. The next time he saw Darius face to face three years later, his enemy lay dead and wrapped in chains, having been stabbed by the fickle supporters that left his corpse in the back of a mud-spattered, overturned donkey cart. The burning of the Hundred Columned Hall at Persepolis in that same year has often been characterised as the regrettable aftermath of a drunken revel, but may instead have

ABOVE: Phaselis, site plan; BELOW: Gordion, site plan

been a spectacular and premeditated act of frustration carried out upon the most visible symbol of Persian atrocities against the Greeks in the past. If so, this uncharacteristic act was the logical counterpart of the burning of the Parthenon two centuries earlier. It has been said of Alexander that if conflicts did not exist to challenge him, he would have created them in his constant need for confrontation. In the final seven years of his life following the battle of Gaugamela and the burning of Persepolis, he penetrated further and further into previously unknown territory, always seeking the definitive personal test that never came, and finding instead that he had expanded the horizons of Hellenism far beyond his wildest expectations. Accounts of his remarkable accomplishment, while divergent in many details because of fragmentary original accounts, all convey the growing sense of mission that slowly began to emerge from his personal crusade and an expanding belief in the possibility of uniting two separate worlds.

After these highly charged rituals at Troy and his subsequent victory at the Granicus to the north, Alexander made his circuitous way through what is now Turkey along a path that was determined by both strategic and fiscal considerations. This serpentine route, which was far from comprehensive because of the vast scope of the area to be covered as well as the variety and rugged topography of the land, began in a southerly direction from The Troad, somewhat inland from the Aegean coast through the province of Lydia. Once through this area, the army turned eastwards at Halicarnassos and followed the line of the Mediterranean towards Perge, after which it turned northwards towards the Anatolian interior and the city of Gordion. Here it waited for badly needed reinforcements coming across the Hellespont from Macedon, and once reinforced, Alexander continued onwards into central Anatolia once again, passing through Ancyra, or today's Ankara, which is now the capital of Turkey. From there he turned south along the outer fringe of the wasteland of Cappadocia then to pass through the Cilician Gates in the Taurus mountains, arriving at a second appointment with Darius at the battle of Issus, near Antioch, on the first of November, 333 BC.

In the course of this march, large portions of central Anatolia and Cappadocia were missed out, as was the entire Black Sea coast and that portion of Mediterranean Cilicia between Perge and Tarsus. Cities with more deeply-rooted Hellenic connections in the past, either as colonies or in political sentiment, seemed to be the preferred destinations of his expedition. Sardis, as one of the first of the cities that Alexander sought out after moving south from Troy, had a mythical attraction as well as strong political ties to the Hellenic West. As the very real creation of the far from mythical Croesus, the city was still the royal seat of Lydia at this time. Stories of the vast wealth of the city in the past must undoubtedly have held some appeal for Alexander but such stories paled in comparison to the legendary liaison that had produced the Heraklean line from which Croesus himself initially claimed descent. This love story, which linked Alexander's famous Argead ancestor with the Lydian queen Omphale, had captured the imagination of many artists at the time, and almost certainly attracted the curiosity of the young king himself. The Sardis that he would have seen was very similar to the city that Croesus had known and was surprisingly large; with a population of nearly 150,000 people when the expedition entered it.[17] The end of the reign of Croesus in 547 BC had marked the start of the Persian occupation of Asia Minor, just as Alexander's invasion had marked its completion. During these two centuries of occupation, the Persians had developed the city into an important western

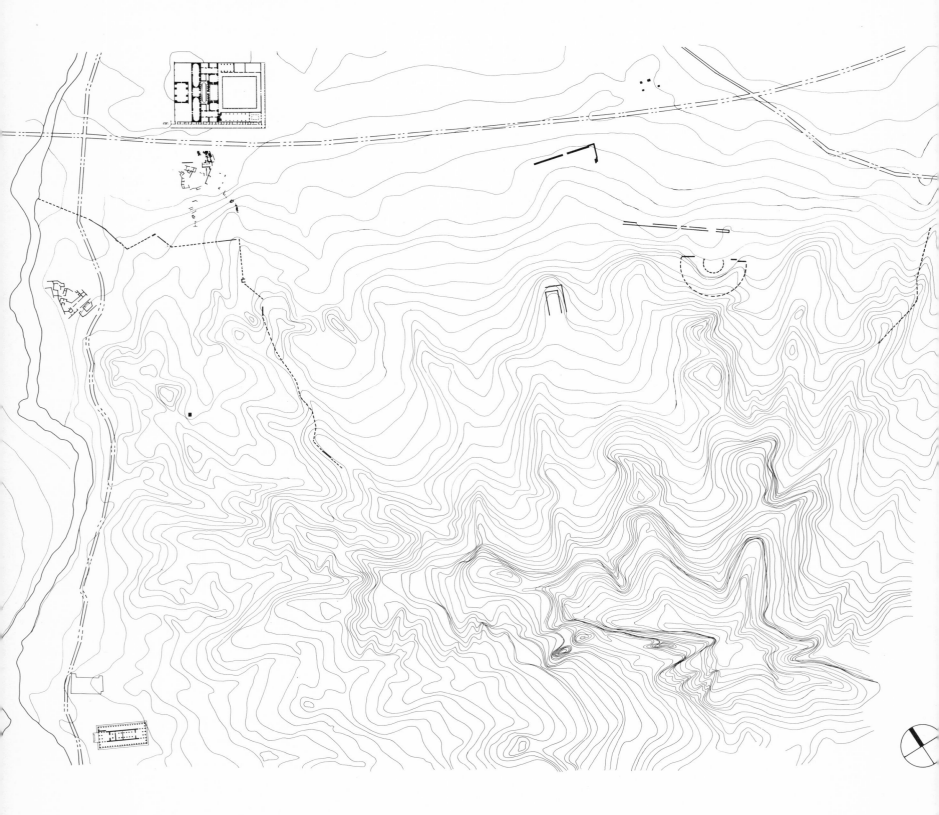

Sardis, site plan

terminus on the royal road from Susa and a key part of their regional plan for the area. Their broad, regional view, which filtered down to a satrapal system of government, and was dramatically different from the Greek habit of isolated city states, must have impressed a leader who had heretofore been struggling against the compartmentalised mentality of the polis, as had his father Philip before him. In spite of the great Persian advances in this region, however, Anatolia remained, as it has been called, 'a country of old and primitive rites'.[18] The persistence of these rites, and the survival of intricately layered social patterns gave Sardis and all of the other cities that Alexander encountered a curiously ambivalent character.

As the seemingly inexorable process of Hellenisation continued to spread in Asia Minor following Alexander's year-long trek across Anatolia, Greek cities proliferated and their founding seemed to have been one of his most cherished royal prerogatives. To be fair, it was a prerogative first used extensively by his father Philip, who felt that the city was the most noble creation of a king and also the most effective device for holding territory. The cities that Alexander supposedly founded throughout the East are sufficient testimony to what Robin Lane Fox has called 'his most lasting contribution to history'.[19] His desire to establish cities was initially based on the certainty that the Persians were 'barbarians', for who else but a barbarian would be capable of sacking sacred Athens and burning down the Parthenon? Like Coventry Cathedral or the Hiroshima tower in the present day, the desecrated shell of the temple was purposely left untouched for centuries so that all could see and remember the unthinkable atrocity that had been committed by a hated enemy. Such views were also continuously alluded to in intellectual circles, particularly by Alexander's tutor Aristotle, who most certainly transmitted them to the young King. In his *Politics*, for example, Aristotle has written that 'It is meet that barbarous peoples should be governed by the Greeks'.[20]

As Alexander began to develop a deeper understanding of and appreciation for the people he had conquered, such prejudices were slowly transformed into an admiration for a society that he found to be extremely complex and refined. While the oligarchies that the Persians had imposed upon the subject cities of Asia Minor, as elsewhere, were abhorrent to his democratic ideals, Alexander began to consider a policy of fusion between the cultures, combined with a relentless promotion of Hellenic social forms. The purpose of this twin initiative was not only to hold on to the territory he had just won, but also to encourage trade and the increased flow of revenue from the incredibly wealthy East towards the impoverished Greek West. Only the foundation of cities, not merely as military garrisons but as functioning urban entities, could satisfy all of these goals. There was certainly no shortage of potential citizens available to settle into each of the new cities that he wished to establish. Scattered Greek populations had existed throughout Asia Minor for some time, and these supplemented by colonists from the mainland seeking relief from the harsh economic conditions there, were also augmented by the ranks of soldiers retiring from Alexander's army. Together, all of these formed the nucleus of the new urban centres. The soldiers were especially effective in providing the military might necessary to protect the new cities from all comers, especially considering the toughness of the Macedonian veterans who have been historically credited with almost superhuman strength. The regimented military background of the majority of these new settlers also added a novel dimension to the governmental systems set up in these cities which were basically organised according to the principles used in Athens at that time.

After Alexander, the entire concept of monarchy was never to be the same again. His breadth of vision and personal style greatly affected the behaviour of his successors, as well as the Roman emperors that followed them, such as Caesar, Augustus, Caracalla, and Hadrian, who sought to re-create the empire that he had won. He was in a very real sense the first political leader to recognise that he was playing to an international audience, and that his actions could be effectively enhanced by changes in his image. His gestures were admittedly larger than life not because he suffered from a blind megalomania, but because he was sensitive to the scrutiny of the many diverse cultural views of the world he sought to unite. For this reason, he always included the local gods in the habitual sacrifices performed in each new area that he visited and also, at least initially, tried to keep power in the hands of local officials wherever possible. His dress, mannerisms, and highly personal, aggressive style of leadership, were at once a genuine part of his character as well as a calculated image carefully constructed for public consumption; to be incrementally altered as his ambitions evolved. While he was the first ruler of the times even to come close to the Platonic ideal of the philosopher–king, he was still also very much a product of the ethos of armed struggle and valour put forward in his beloved *Iliad*. His imaginative and highly aggressive military tactics, combined with the new Greek advances in siege warfare, significantly escalated the level and force of armed conflict throughout the Hellenistic Age. They had a marked impact upon civic defences; particularly in the construction of elaborate walls throughout Asia Minor. Because a smooth succession to power was virtually unknown in Macedon, as was dramatically shown by Alexander's efforts to grasp and keep it when his father Philip was assassinated, his own rightful heirs were not guaranteed kingship when he died. His own words to his followers on his deathbed, when asked who should succeed him, reinforced the typical attitude towards royal inheritance at the time. By saying that his kingdom should go to 'the strongest', he not only gave his sons the same chance at power that he had had should either of them be fit enough to seize it, but also left the door wide open for others to undo all that he had achieved. While he had, through personal example, virtually institutionalised personal involvement and courageous leadership as a king, he was powerless to control the chaos that followed in his wake.

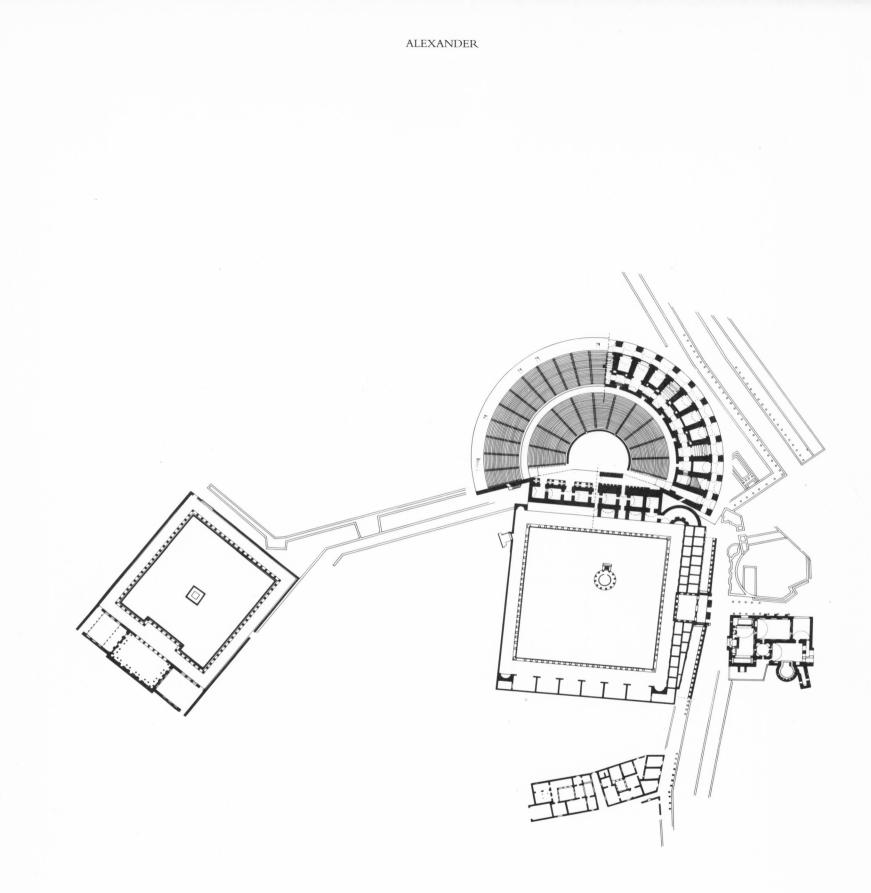

Side, plan of auditorium and agora

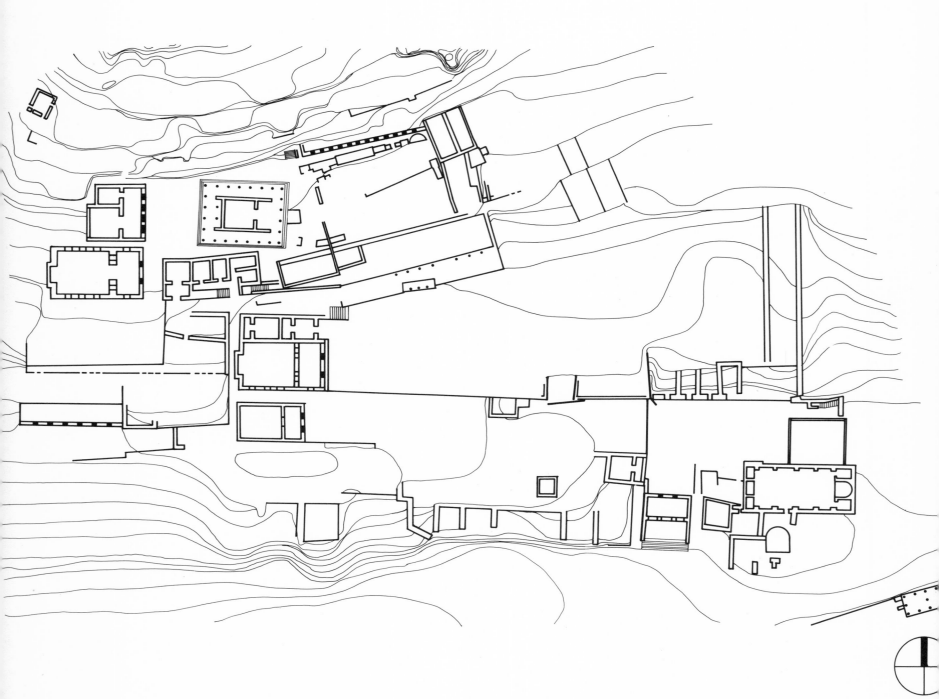

Labranda, site plan

THE SUCCESSORS

Upon Alexander's death, those closest to him lost no time in staking out their individual claims to the most select pieces of the unified world he had fought so hard to achieve. While none among them were as desperate for immortality, nor as enlightened or even as blessed with martial intuition, there were those who shared a bit of his lively intellect as well as his belief in the ultimate wisdom of a union between East and West. Lacking the royal imperative and seemingly limitless resources of their leader, however, these men, such as his secretary Eumenes, or Seleucus, who had been the leader of his shield bearers, faced the resistance and open hostility of a military establishment that had resented such ecumenical efforts from the start, but had been silenced by the sheer power of Alexander's personality. As a Greek from Cardia, Eumenes suffered the additional liability of not even sharing Macedonian kinship. In spite of some impressive tactical gains in his attempt to preserve the Argead dynasty, and Alexander's dream of a united world empire, he was ultimately betrayed by his own troops and turned over to his rival, Antigonus, to be executed in 316 BC. Without another champion to fight for their cause, all of Alexander's house were doomed, and the tragic litany of their destruction speaks volumes about the coldly brutal aspect of an age that was also capable of such high ideals. In a desperate attempt to survive, Alexander's mother, Olympias, made a bold move of her own to protect the dynasty by killing Philip III Arridaeus, who was Philip II's half-witted son by another of his wives, and by massacring more than a hundred followers of Cassander, who was then making a claim upon the Macedonian throne.

In retaliation, Olympias was besieged inside a fortress at Pydna and starved to death, along with her entire retinue. Having disposed of her, Cassander then turned to Alexander's Persian widow, Roxana, and their twelve-year-old son, Alexander IV, whom he first imprisoned in Amphipolis and then murdered in 309 BC. A second son by Barsine, named Herakles, was also killed, as was Alexander's sister, Cleopatra, who was caught in Sardis en route to sanctuary in Egypt. For the next thirty-five years, the men who had followed Alexander to the ends of the earth engaged in a savage bloodbath that has no precedent in the ancient world, and began a long series of struggles that have been carefully documented by historians such as WW Tarn, among others.[1] One of the best generals in history, who commanded so many loyalties and protected countless subjects in life, had ironically provided no safeguards for his own family in the event of his death and, in fact, had almost guaranteed their destruction by his own personal quest for power. Of all the men, including the Macedonians, who had fought at his side, only Eumenes, with his Greek sensibilities seemed fully to comprehend his real intentions, and be able to see through his personal pyrotechnics to the pan-Hellenic ideals that he had believed in.

When the dust had settled and the minor players had been eliminated, Ptolemy, Seleucus,

Antigonus and Attalus had emerged as the four main leaders of the Hellenistic world. Their highly distinct personalities were almost perfectly reflected in the individual kingdoms that they established.

Ptolemy has often been judged by many to have been the wisest of all in his choice of Egypt as a base, primarily because of the long-standing respect for monarchy that had been ingrained there and in the subsequent east of the governing country for thousands of years. This apparent governmental stability, as well as a relatively predictable economy and easily defensible natural borders, made Egypt the ideal choice among all the territorial possibilities that were then open to any of the Successors. Ptolemy I, however, who had served as one of Alexander's generals, took no chances and did not simply rely upon his 'spear won' claim to the Egyptian throne. In addition to taking an Egyptian wife of royal blood to assure his legitimacy in a way that had traditionally been accepted in that country, Ptolemy also intercepted Alexander's catafalque on its way from Babylon to Macedon so that the body might be buried in the centre of the newly-founded Alexandria within his jurisdiction. Searching for other ways to legitimatise his symbolic ties with the fallen king, he also mimicked the past journeys that Alexander had made to both Siwa and Didyma in an attempt to confer upon himself the same divine mandate that the dead king had claimed.[2]

In as many ways as possible, then, Ptolemy tried, and ultimately succeeded, in his attempt to establish the most stable kingdom in the Succession. At the onset, Ptolemy continued to maintain claims on foreign territory that included such diverse areas as the Cyclades, the islands of Samos, Lesbos and Samothrace, and the entire coast of Asia Minor below Ephesus, all the way to Calycadmus. In addition, his entire dynasty intermittently gained and lost control of territories as far north as the Hellespont, including Phrygia, Thrace, southern Syria and Phoenicia up to the Lebanon. In a series of debilitating struggles called 'The Syrian Wars' that began in 276 and continued until 241 BC, this entire region changed hands repeatedly. When they ended, these wars conclusively established the northernmost boundary between the Ptolemaic and Seleucid Empires at the Eleutherus River, which provided a natural dividing line between them. Before this active foreign policy was abandoned, which is generally agreed to have occurred after the reign of Ptolemy III, Egypt seemed to thrive economically, and capitalised on the rapidly expanding trade that was made possible by the more flexible attitude of the Hellenistic Age. Such initial improvement is not difficult to visualise, however, given the moribund state of the country before Ptolemy took control, being worn out as it was by great age and the uncertainties of war. The largely agricultural economy and vast temple estates that the Greeks found there initially benefitted a great deal from their energetic managerial skills, before the inevitable inertia of the country took over. The new colonists, who numbered a mere half a million amidst an estimated ten million Egyptians, did have an undisputed effect upon the economy of their adopted homeland primarily in the expansion of the area of arable land within it, as well as upon the crop yields, which gradually increased. This bounty did not only apply to traditional local crops such as wheat, but also to new varieties that the Greeks introduced. While there were exceptions, such as a failure to transplant olives, there were some spectacular successes, such as grapes, which relieved the homesickness of the Greek expatriates. The reasonably drinkable wine that is found in what is now Egypt had its beginnings in the cuttings that were introduced during the Hellenistic period, and is not called 'Ptolemy' simply by chance. The new settlement of Arsinatis, near Lake Fayum, was one of the most dramatic examples of this novel ingenuity in agricultural planning. Large areas of desert were reclaimed there through the use of extensive irrigation. The lake itself, which had always been the preferred hunting preserve of the Pharaohs (as is shown on many of the wall paintings in the tombs of the Valleys of the Kings and the Queens in Luxor), still attracts waterfowl of all types, in the migratory flights to and from Africa. The lush palm groves, fig and olive orchards and grape arbours planted by the Greeks, however, have long since disappeared, and the forlorn temples which still exist there and are now surrounded by the insistent sands are all that remain as a reminder of their brief period of glory. In addition to these new improvements in agriculture, many long-neglected trade routes, such as those across the Red Sea to the Hijaz, or south to Ethiopia, and westward to the Aegean Coast of Asia Minor and the Attic mainland, were reopened, and an inefficient system of bartering was abandoned in favour of the currency then commonly in use throughout the Mediterranean. A peculiar and surprising bonus provided by this adopted homeland was the availability of elephants, whose strategic importance in Alexander's last battles in India had left an indelible impression upon all of his generals. The first three Ptolemaic rulers took advantage of supplies near at hand in the Sudan to supplement their army, as well as taking advantage of the economics of offering them up for sale.[3] Eventually, however, the initial spurt of energy provided by this relatively small group of colonists began to be slowed by the inertia of centuries of bureaucracy, and the basic cultural differences between the two peoples began to emerge. For thousands of years before the Ptolemaic intrusion into their affairs, the Egyptians had regarded their Pharaoh as a divine being who had the unquestioned right to claim all of their land as his own. This theocratic ownership also extended to the people themselves and their stewardship of the land. Their constant care and maintenance of the intricate system of ditches and dams that were used to divert the annual floods into the thin band of green fields surrounding the river were essential for the survival of everyone that depended upon the fragile ecosystem of the Nile Valley for a livelihood. Castes of priests and scribes and courtiers grew up alongside the aloof and distant god-king, whom the people felt allowed this mysterious liquid gift to occur and their power unfortunately continued to grow. As they began to do more and more of the actual work of running the government, their influence began to become so strong that it even challenged that of the Pharaoh, in some cases. The duality that was inherent in this situation inevitably led to protective duplicity, as well as a burgeoning amount of records kept by each of the separate factions struggling to gain control over a remote and increasingly isolated ruler.

The Greeks, on the other hand, were of a more independent mind and were far from unaware of these internal conflicts. Having typically come from an individual polis, or city state of moderate size, each of them had either had an active or tacit role in the governing of their city. The economy of each polis was determined by both its specific geographic circumstances, in relation to its agricultural potential and the availability of specialised products and trading partners, as well as its physical size and the number of its citizens. When confronted with the vast scale and rigidly established patterns of Egypt, the Greek tendency was to attempt to apply the rational and orderly thought processes used in a much more comprehensible system to a culture and bureaucracy that appeared to them to be in chaos. The overall effect of the economic application of the same relentless logic that had been used

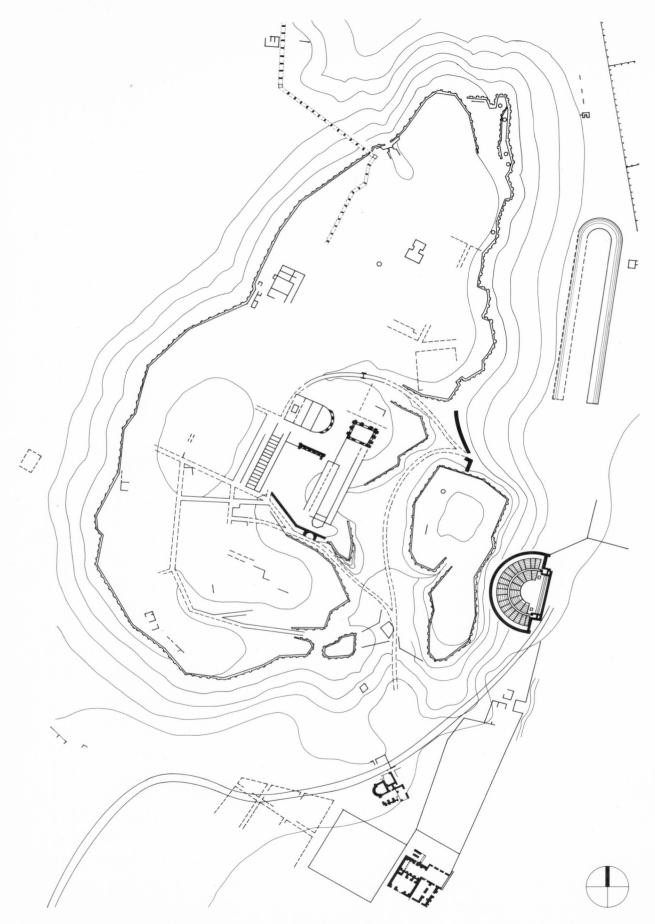

Aspendos, site plan

by philosophers like Socrates to badger his students, when grafted onto a long tradition of blind obedience to an all powerful, but secretly manipulated sovereign, was effectively to distance the common working man even further from the government's purpose. As was also the case in the Tigris and Euphrates River valleys, Egypt's agricultural base had initially been the main reason for the precocious development of such a sophisticated culture there, because the organisation skills required to regulate, grow, store and sell the crops that were produced, were also those required to administer the cities that were the cornerstone of culture itself. As with any system of administration, however, the records that were required to keep track of everyday transactions began to multiply and become extremely complicated. The alien system of regulations that the Greeks then layered over this existing condition must have severely tested the tolerance of the Egyptian people.

The key to the new system was the concept of a centralised administration that acted as a hub for forty districts, or *nomes*. These, in turn, were ruled by a governor, or *strategus*, and a scribe that assisted in the keeping of records. Each of the districts were further subdivided into *toparchies* administered by a *toparch* and his scribe, called a *topogrammateus*. Each toparch was made up of the individual village units that were the backbone of the Egyptian economy, and each had a *comarch*, or leader, and the ubiquitous *comogrammateus*, or scribe that kept the village records. Each of these administrators, as well as all of the members of their staff, were appointed by the king, and were ultimately responsible to him. As AHM Jones has said: 'Such a system was expensive and needed careful supervision, but if it was efficiently run . . . it made possible the most minute and elaborate economic exploitation of the country in the interest of the government. In Egypt this exploitation went to extraordinary lengths.'[4] The novel office of the 'tax farmer', which the Ptolemies also introduced into Egypt, served to make the burden on the taxpayer there even more unbearable. Through it, the right to levy taxes was distributed to the highest bidder, who in turn guaranteed the crown the tax revenue that was estimated to be required. How much additional revenue was extracted, and the means used to get it, were never questioned. While beneficial for both the crown and the collectors, this system only served to further alienate the people from their rulers.[5]

The zeal with which such new administrative devices were introduced was also borne of a certain urgency, due to the Ptolemaic awareness of the economic potential of their adopted country, and their need to establish a firm position within it. That position was also dependent upon military strength, and the second goal of the new government became the transformation of the rich surplus of agricultural goods and exotic products that were available to them into the raw materials and weapons needed to sustain an army and wage war. Of all of the crops grown in Egypt, wheat remained the most spectacular agricultural success. Biblical accounts of this region constantly allude to the bountiful harvests there, as well as the adverse consequences that befell the entire Mediterranean basin when a late or minimal flooding of the Nile resulted in an inadequate yield. The export of wheat in years of surplus not only brought a great deal of income into Egypt, but also established patterns of dependence, as countries such as Macedon and mainland Greece began to rely increasingly upon this steady source of food. This dependence gave the Ptolemies a great deal of power over their neighbours, and their intentional policy of what has been termed 'economic imperialism' was effective against their rivals until later abandoned in favour of isolationism.[6]

In contrast to the highly controlled and agriculturally based kingdom of the Ptolemies, the Seleucids did not have the advantage of such easily defensible borders, and the constant threats to their territory forced them to use up enormous financial resources on the military campaigns that were needed to retain sovereignty. While the Ptolemies sought to graft their royal authority upon that of the Pharaohs, the Seleucids depended upon the mystical caches of the Achaemenids, and the past glory of Babylon as their source of power.[7] Seleucus himself, as the founder of the dynasty, had been the only one of the Successors that did not divorce the Persian wife he had married at the ecumenical ceremony at Susa. He alone, of all the Successors, continuously showed a deeper understanding of Alexander's controversial attempts to link the cultures of East and West. While the mixed blood of his sons gave them far greater authority in their chosen region, they did not rely upon heredity alone for power but continued to strengthen their cultural claims through the consistent encouragement of science and the arts. In addition to the revival of history and literature, ancient myths and the Babylonian discoveries in astronomy were also codified, as well as the music and ancient religious rituals of the region.[8]

After Seleucus had firmly established a base of power in Babylon in 312 BC, he attempted to move against India as well but finally realised the futility of his aspirations there and abandoned them around 303. His kingdom, however, did expand to include what is now northern Syria and Mesopotamia by 301, and finally took in most of Asia Minor, with the exception of several stubbornly resistant enclaves, by 281. His son, Antiochus, as the grandson of the Persian satrap Spitamenes, commanded even more loyalty in the Mesopotamian region than his father had done, and controlled an empire that extended from the Aegean to Turkestan. The Seleucids, through nearly continuous military action and high political intrigue, managed to keep the majority of this kingdom intact until it was gradually diminished by the Bactrians and Parthians, and then finally lost to Rome in 189. In spite of their defeat by Rome, however, they continued to hold Cilicia and most of the Mediterranean coast of Asia Minor, as well as Babylon and Judea, for sixty more years. In the course of nearly two centuries of their rule, the Seleucids developed three highly identifiable urban centres that they depended upon in equal measure to control their far flung kingdom.[9] The first of these was Sardis which has already been cited as one of the first of Alexander's stops on his way through Asia Minor to the East. Sardis had traditionally been the western terminus of the ancient Persian royal road which began in Susa, and which was so vital to the maintenance of the communications, military manoeuvres and trade that held distant borders of their empire together. Because of its importance as a political, religious and economic focal point in western Asia Minor, Sardis was the logical choice as the keystone of Seleucid policy there. Unlike the second centre of Antioch, or the third at Babylon, Sardis was critical to the control of an intricate network of regions, such as Phrygia, Lydia, Caria, Cilicia, and southern Cappadocia, as well as acting as a bulwark against Ptolemaic expansion out of bases in Lycia and Pamphylia, nearby. In addition to these three main centres, the Seleucids also enacted an active policy of colonisation, and used the establishment of new settlements as a form of urban imperialism that suited their precarious circumstances much better than the economic version practised by the Ptolemies in Egypt. As an indication of the energy and financial resources expended by the Seleucids in these colonisation efforts, Seleucus Nicator alone is credited with the foundation of sixteen

Antiochs, nine Seleucias, six Laodiceas, three Apameaes, and a Stratonicea, scattered throughout Mesopotamia, and the border region between northern Syria and Cilicia.[10]

Many of these Seleucid settlements vanished in the same way that those founded by Alexander did, but several of them took root and continued to have a stabilising influence over a long period of time. This was especially true in northern Syria, with cities such as the dynastic necropolis at Seleucia in Pieria, or Latakiyeh, or Beroea on the Chalus, which is now known as Aleppo. By 148 BC these particular cities considered themselves to be so similar in all respects that they fused their monetary systems into one. The economic and cultural development of many of these urban centres, as well as their financial prosperity, offers clear testimony to the differences between the Seleucid and Ptolemaic philosophy of rule. Where the Ptolemies, after the third ruler in their line, became passive and economically insular within their secure borders, the Seleucids, of necessity, became more politically and militarily active in their dealings with their constantly threatening neighbours, as well as more *laissez-faire* in their economic policies. Such activity was essential in order to rule a diverse kingdom that held nearly thirty million subjects at its maximum extent, of which only one million were the Greeks concentrated mainly along the Aegean coast of Asia Minor.[11] For the remainder, the retention of the administrative and religious forms of the Achaemenids proved to be quite popular and politically expedient, and far more realistic than Alexander's lofty but ultimately impotent visions of concord.

In stark contrast to either the systematic governmental control exercised by the Ptolemies, or the *laissez-faire* attitude of the Seleucids, the Antigonid dynasty in Macedon consistently retained their own time-tested system of allowing semi-autonomous communities to occupy the central plain, and tribal groups to retain their traditional lands in the western hills.[12] This arrangement seemed to be very well adapted to the independent temperament of the various factions involved, as demonstrated by the fact that the Antigonids were able to retain overall control of Greece itself until 196 BC and continued on in Macedon until 168. Opinions differ widely regarding conditions in Alexander's homeland following this epic crusade towards the East, ranging from estimates of only thirty thousand men withdrawn from Macedon, to those who speculate on the total depopulation of all males of military age and the subsequent destruction of the country's agriculturally based economy. If the later estimates are true, Alexander would have ironically gained his fame, as well as having made possible the wider expectations of the Hellenistic Age, at the expense of the well-being of Greece and Macedon itself.

In the midst of all of this violence and competition for territory, a remarkable civic phenomenon then occurred on the Aegean coast of Asia Minor. Seeking a safe place to put the enormous treasure he had amassed on his campaigns with Alexander, Lysimachus settled on the natural citadel of Pergamon to hide it, just prior to being defeated and executed by Seleucus at Corupedion, in Lydia, in 281 BC. He had designated a man named Philtaerus as the guardian of the treasure, and after the death of the general, Philtaerus frantically tried in every way possible to bide time so that the local alliances could be formed that would allow him to keep the bequest and fortify the citadel still further. Dissembling in ways that would easily rival Penelope's delay of her suitors, Philtaerus successfully deflected the Seleucid claims to the fortune, and continued to expand his new city around the

Pergamon, site plan

Acropolis where the treasure had originally been stored. In order to ensure the continued growth of the city he had begun to develop, Philtaerus named his nephew Eumenes as his successor prior to his own death in 263. Eumenes proved equal to the task, and in addition to successfully resisting the continuous attacks of the Seleucids, and others, he managed to build on the work his uncle had completed by expanding both the scope and territory of the fledgling city. Upon the succession of Attalus I to the Pergamene throne in 241 BC, the kingdom had finally become well established as a strong, independent principality in its own right, in the midst of the claims and counterclaims then being made on the other parts of Asia Minor that surrounded it.

During the brief period of its ascendency, from the death of Lysimachus in 281, until its bequest to Rome in 133 by Attalus III, Pergamon evolved into what may arguably be considered one of the finest examples of a Hellenistic city. As such, it offers a valid, and diametrically opposite counterpoint to a Classical Greek polis, such as Athens, in both its form and self-image, and provides a valuable example with which to compare the two historical periods.

In its most prosperous era, Athens certainly offers one of the best models of the Classical Greek polis, or independent city state, as it could easily provide its citizens with all of their physical and spiritual needs. As the patron goddess of the city, Athena Polias represented far more than a tangible version of a natural force. She was, instead, the personification of the city itself, and represented the highest aspirations that its citizens had of urban life. *Civitas*, in its most basic sense, conveys the idea of people gathering together in one place in order to co-operate against the natural dangers that surround them, and the polis itself began to grow in direct proportion to its role as protector and provider for them. Like many other Classical Greek cities of its time, Athens also had the double core of *agora* and *acropolis* that resulted from the pragmatic division of the commercial and sacred aspects of urban life. The Athenian agora, in the first century of its growth, quickly evolved from a rather disorderly enfilade of buildings strung along the bottom of a low ridge behind it, to an incrementally formed parallelogram of municipal and commercial structures that were deliberately placed to enhance both the delight of those moving through it and gathering within it.[13] One of the most critical determinants of the form of both the agora and acropolis, in this regard, was the traditional path of the Panathenaic procession, in which all of the people of the city joined together in an annual reaffirmation of their civic pledge to remain loyal to the place that offered them sanctuary. The Parthenon, as the home of Athena Polias and the architectural representation of the city, was the final goal of this procession, which has been immortalised on a frieze carved on the inner fascia of the building. The placement of the Parthenon, as well as the location and locale of each of the other buildings around it therefore had a profound meaning for all of the participants in the Panathenaia, especially as it emerged in rising view through the frame of the Propylaea gate. The angles of the Parthenon on the right, and the Erectheon on the left, when seen through this frame, subliminally guided the view of those approaching the Acropolis towards a statue of Athena that once stood between them and which was placed on a projecting terrace to make it even more prominent. Such framed views were certainly not unique to Athens, as has been shown by the research of Constantine Doxiades. In addition to his survey of the direct geometrical relationship between the angle of vision of a viewer standing at the Propylaea Gate and the corners of each of the buildings on the Athenian

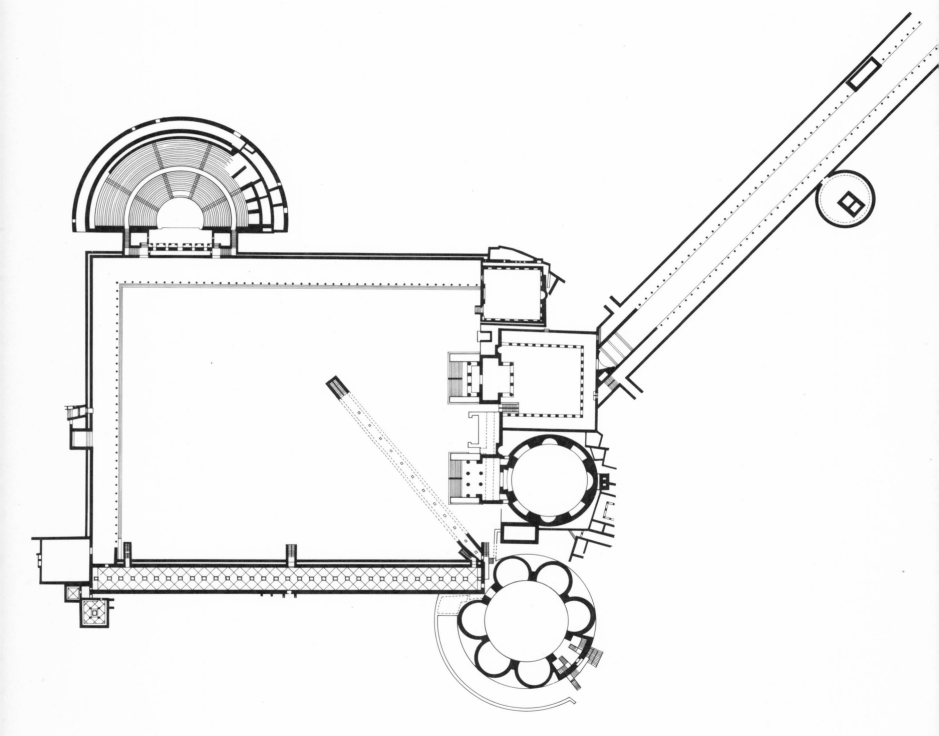

Plan of Asklepeion, Pergamon

acropolis, Doxiades has gone on to test his theory of visual criteria as a form generator in many other Greek cities as well, with equally impressive results.[14] The intricate relationship of all of the buildings on the Athenian acropolis, then, as finally realised by Pericles, Ictinus, Callicrates and Phydias in 432 BC, shows an intentional attempt to generate both a religious and civic experience through the sequential placement of objects in space.

Just two centuries later, however, the design of Pergamon shows that all of these considerations had changed, and the architectonic link between the people and their city had been irrevocably altered. Due to the unique circumstances behind its rapid rise to prominence and the need for the city to become quickly a viable political entity among the other fragmented factions then vying for power, Pergamon did not have the luxury of a slow, formal evolution, as Athens did. During its greatest phase of growth, which coincided with the thirty-eight year reign of King Eumenes II, the new city not only had to deal with severe topographical challenges, but also answer to the concurrent demands of the commercial zone at the bottom of the citadel and the protective requirements of the palaces surrounding the treasury at its peak. Pergamon tended to grow in two directions at once, expanding into terraces of various widths that were cut into the steep mountainside; spanning between the acropolis and the lower city at its base. In vivid contrast to Athens, the highest priority in Pergamon is not given to the icon of a deity that is also a metaphor of the city itself, but to the stronghold of a king and the wealth that made his power possible. As in the Bronze Age, the external form of the city of Pergamon once more evolved in a full circle, into an expression of people living under the rule of a king, and not a god.

There was also a statue of Athena at Pergamon, but rather than serving as the dramatic finale to a reverent procession, as it did in Athens, it was located on a terrace that was cut into the middle of the mountainside, about halfway between the lower city and the acropolis. Rather than being surrounded by the houses of the gods, and the mausoleums of ancestors, this statue served as the focal point of an open courtyard and the library which enclosed it, showing the extent to which the search for knowledge had begun to replace traditional religious values in the Hellenistic Age. The temple of Dionysus, which may be considered the real counterpart of the Athenian Parthenon in this city, built in the second century BC, formed the terminus of a long, thin shelf created in front of the library and the theatre directly adjacent to it. The narrow, man-made ledge on which it sat was held up by a long retaining wall, strengthened by thick buttresses along its entire length, which only tended to accentuate the linear movement towards the temple at the far end, and punctuate the distance. Rather than being displayed in three-quarter perspective, as the Parthenon in Athens is, this small building was only visible in full-front elevation, once those intending to worship there were locked into the entrance procession that they were intended to follow. The size of the building no longer allowed access to the interior, but restricted worship to the grand stairway leading up to its facade. As with the statue of Athena nearby, the Temple of Dionysus at Pergamon clearly proclaims a change in social values, in which form overtakes content and appearances take on great importance.

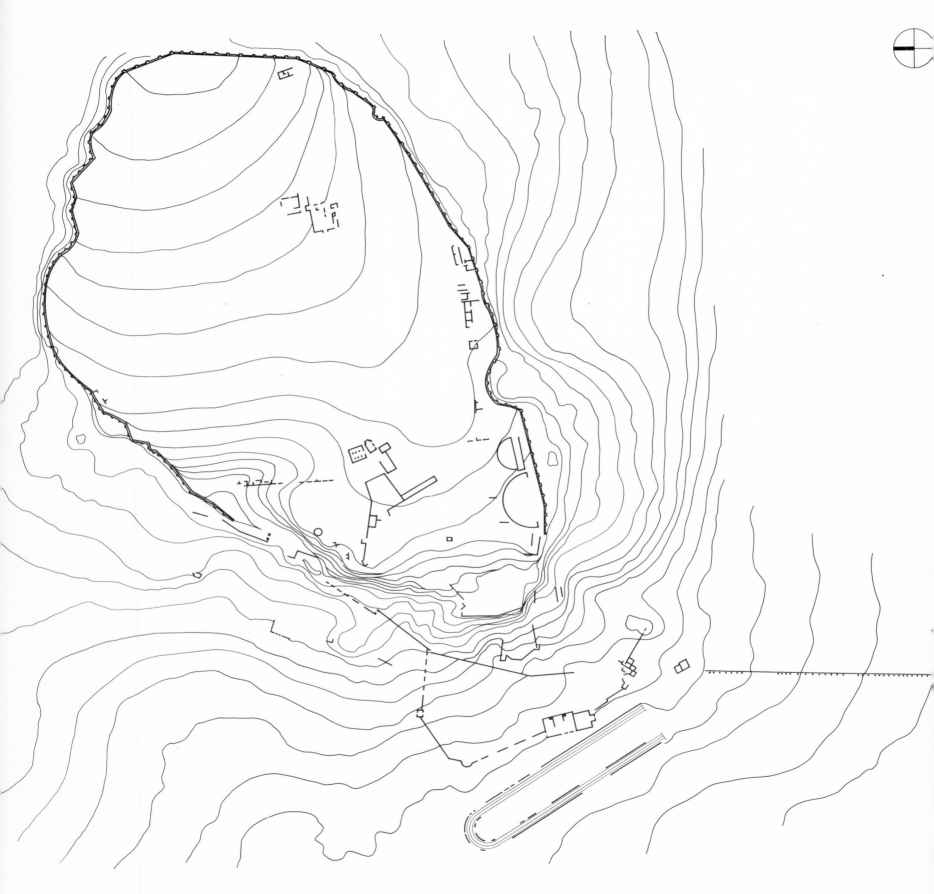

Sillyon, site plan

THE CITIES

I f they are given any credence at all in histories of ancient Greece, the cities in Asia Minor are usually relegated to a secondary position of influence and treated as the grateful beneficiary of the unparalleled cultural strides made on the mainland in Attica. The truth is quite the opposite, as many of the intellectual and philosophical innovations that made this progress possible are known to have originated in Asia Minor, and then to have moved West. The litany of these influences, while not widely known, is extensive, and has been recited in several other sources.[1] The important point to reiterate, however, is that these innovations were not of a superficial nature, but penetrate to the very heart of the Hellenic ethos.

Ionia, which was the central region of the Aegean coastline of Asia Minor that separated Aeolia on the north from Caria on the south, originally took its name from a quasi-mythical patriarch named Ion. While he is conventionally listed as having been the son of an early Athenian King named Xuthus and Queen Creusa, and of having led a colonisation effort from Athens to Asia Minor in the wake of the Dorian invasions of 1120 BC, there are less well-known and extremely tantalising variations of this foundation myth. While most sources agree about the four Ionian tribes that grew out of the four sons of Ion, named Geleontes, Argadeis, Aigikareis, and Hopletes, another less well-known genealogy places the origin of Ion much further to the East. In the biblical 'Tale of Nations' in *Genesis*, it states that: 'This is the account of Shem, Ham and Japeth, Noah's sons, who themselves had sons after the flood. The sons of Japeth (were) Gomer, Magog, Madai, Javan, Tubal, Meshech and Tiras . . . The sons of Javan (were) Elishah, Tarshish, Kittim, and Dodanim. From these, the maritime peoples spread out into their territories by their clans within their nations, each with their own language.'[2] In his overview of the Asiatic elements in Greek civilisation, Sir William Ramsay had raised the point that the Greek version of Javan is Ion, and it is also interesting to note that the area strongly indicated by tradition as the starting point for Noah's flock is Mount Ararat in eastern Anatolia.[3] Whatever the true origin of Ion was, the region of Ionia in Asia Minor is most likely to have been the birthplace of the poet Homer, whose *Iliad* and *Odyssey* both had an incalculable impact upon Hellenic religion, mythology and social values.

While several Ionian cities have laid claim to this honour, the island of Chios, which is about five miles from the Turkish coastline, is widely acknowledged to have been his home, as well as the location of a group of his disciplines called the Homeridae, who perpetuated his poems through recitation until they were finally codified around 750 BC.[4] While the dramatic events that Homer speaks about were probably derived from a cataclysm that took place at Troy around 1195 BC, those that feel that he alone composed *The Iliad*, also believe that he did so about 1000 BC. Once called 'the Bible of Hellenism', *The Iliad* was such an essential part of early Greek education that it was memorised verbatim and recited aloud in much the same way that Koranic verses are recited in Islamic schools today.[5] As in the current example cited, such readings were not only intended to teach the basic skills of spelling and reading, but were also considered to be an effective way of inculcating the basic values that are contained in the verse. In the case of *The Iliad*, those values revolved around the importance of personal courage, valour and honour and were presented in such a way as to stress continually the degree of human frailty in comparison to the immortality of the gods. Homer, as well as Hesiod, personified vividly each deity in the Greek pantheon in such a way that their highly individualised characteristics could be understood by the common man, and easily linked with the natural phenomenon they were meant to embody. As historian Michael Grant has so aptly described this important identification: 'Homer and Hesiod were credited, more plausibly, with the remarkable achievement of standardising and welding together the Olympic gods for Greece (and) Homer in particular makes of them . . . a collection of perilously powerful divinities full of vices and foibles.'[6] Many of the deities in that pantheon originally sprang from Eastern cults. Dionysus, for example, who may have been so instrumental in the rites behind the formation of Greek drama, is known to have had his origins in the worship of Diouns, who was the Phrygian god of vegetation.[7] Other obvious examples are the Greek goddess Artemis, who was derived from the ancient Anatolian mother goddess Kybele, or Cybele, as well as Zeus, who bore a strong resemblance to Kronos, who was the Hittite god of heaven. This later comparison even extends to the wives of these 'fathers of the gods', who were called Hera and Hepat, respectively. Such similarities can be noted for virtually every member of the Olympic pantheon, indicating the degree to which Homer did indeed manage to Hellenise many diverse religious conventions into a single tradition. As Sir William Ramsay has said: 'One remarkable fact strikes every observer, and that is that the personal names in old Greek mythology are rarely Greek.'[8]

With Alexander, and his love of Homer's *Iliad*, then, the influence of Ionia comes around full circle, in that a Macedonian who was more Greek than the Greeks was able to bring Hellenism back to the region where its highest ideals had been formulated in the first place. The generating influence of Ionia in this circle does not stop there, however, but may be said to extend even further to the first Persian incursions into the Aegean area of Asia Minor. Their rule of this area, which followed the capture and sack of Sardis in 546 BC and their eventual conquest of each of the Ionian cities in their turn, was not particularly harsh, and was administered at a distance through a system of local satraps or governors. Yet, even this intrusion was unacceptable, and in 499 BC the Ionians and particularly Aristagoras of Miletus, instigated a revolt to throw the Persians out. Efforts to find allies in this revolt on the mainland were not as successful as originally expected, but Athens did send twenty ships and Eretria sent five.[9] In a naval battle off the island of Lade, which has long since been fused by a field of silt to the place where Miletus once proudly stood overlooking its harbour, the Persians shattered the badly organised confederation and the ensuing destruction of Miletus thus became a foregone conclusion. After this battle in 494 BC, the Persians went on to try to punish those who had assisted the Ionians in their revolt, leading to the famous battle of Marathon in 490. This was followed ten years later by a major Persian expedition that led to the capitulation of Athens and the burning of the Parthenon, which incensed Greeks everywhere. The ensuing formation of the Delian League, with

Miletus, site plan

Athens at its head, and the eventual restoration of that city which led to the Persian defeat at Eurymedon in 467 was not sufficient to erase that blasphemy. In a very real sense, the Hellenic crusade called for by Isocrates was a direct result of the painful memory of that invasion, even though nearly a century and a half had passed between the desecration of the Acropolis and Alexander's crossing of the Dardanelles to free Asia Minor from Persian rule.

Miletus, which had originally initiated this chain of events, also rose from its own ashes, but was never again able to regain the position of leadership that it had had in Ionia prior to the revolt. In the Hellenistic period, however, it did become an extremely active commercial centre once again, and the long and narrow Bay of Lions that diagonally penetrated into the peninsula on which the city was situated, was always alive with the loading and unloading of ships wanting to deliver goods to the agora at its heart. Hippodamus, who has given his name to the gridiron plan which he is thought to have devised to insure the more rapid development of the colonies which the Ionians founded, was also a Milesian, and the orthogonal layout of his own city at this time strongly indicates his influence. Rather than being rigid and confining, however, the grid of Miletus elegantly adapts to the irregular shore line of its peninsular base and easily allows for the incremental expansion of successively wider open spaces that lead from the harbour's edge to the agora in its midst. The freedom that is achieved within this overall grid is an object lesson to all contemporary urban planners who have felt restrained by the device since, and demonstrated the endless permutations that are possible within this repetitive system. As Vincent Scully has described the overall layout of Miletus at this time:

> The city itself might now be conceived of as one balanced, articulated body, but one whose form was more closely related to the conceptualisations of a philosophical system than to the physicalities of a piece of Classical sculpture. In a sense the site of Miletos itself . . . suggests the logic of the Hippodamian three-part division in residential grids on the slightly elevated portions and spacious public areas in the low ground near the harbours in the centre . . . At Miletos the Hippodamian grid may therefore be felt to have liberated the town.[10]

The major buildings typically found in all of the Hellenistic cities of Asia Minor at this time, such as the bouleuterion, gymnasium and theatre, are strategically placed to punctuate the path of movement from harbour to agora, acting as landmarks with the linked spaces that they individually dominate. The Delphinion, which is one of these, is delightfully unique to Miletus. In it, a circular raised altar, which is felt to be the oldest of its type in Asia Minor, has been identified as having been dedicated to Apollo. The name of the temple, taken from the Greek word for Dolphin, confirms this association, as both the god and the dolphins who were the temple's namesake were supposed to be especially responsive to music. Miletus also controlled the shrine of Apollo, which was connected to it by a ten-mile long sacred way that dates from the end of the eighth century BC. The origins and importance of the archaic temple revolved around a natural spring that was located there and interpretations of its rushing and gurgling were later proclaimed to be the oracles of Apollo by the priests of this sacred precinct, which made it an equal to those at both Delos and Delphi.[11] The story of the priests at Didyma, who were called the Branchidae, crosses paths with Alexander's own, in one of the least complimentary and most controversial incidents of his extraordinary campaign. The Branchidae, who had been charged by the Milesians with the protection of the Didyma Temple and its sizeable

Ephesus, site plan

treasury, sided with the Persian King Darius during his invasion of Asia Minor and less than reluctantly turned over the contents of the vault to him.[12] In order to protect his unexpected benefactors from certain death at the hands of any surviving Milesians, Darius relocated them in Bactria, in Central Asia. The spring of Apollo and the oracle of the temple is recorded to have been silent from the time of this robbery and the subsequent burning of the temple, until the arrival of Alexander there in 494 BC. The silence of the oracle was supposedly broken with a proclamation that the 'true son of Zeus and future victor at Gaugamela' had appeared; and the sacred spring began to gush again. When this fresh prophecy came true and Alexander had finally penetrated into Asia as far as Bactria and beyond, the Milesians under his command are recorded in some sources as having demanded the execution of the descendants of the Branchidae that they uncovered. Their probable massacre, along with the death march across the Macran desert and the burning of the palaces of Persepolis may mark the nadir of a brilliant general's career.[13]

While Miletus was politically pre-eminent in Ionia, for an extended period of time, it was certainly not unique in architectural grandeur. The other eleven cities of that region, that made up the pan-Ionian League, such as Smyrna, Ephesus, Priene, or Herakleia among others, may rightly be considered to be comparable to it in that regard, but it was in Miletus that the individualism that came to be the hallmark of the Hellenistic Age began to emerge for the first time.[14]

The Mermnadic dynasty of Lydia, and most particularly king Croesus of that line, effectively blocked all Milesian attempts at eastwards expansion into central Anatolia, and forced them out into the Aegean in a massive colonisation effort that also played a decisive role in the development of Ephesus nearby. Settlement at Ephesus is thought to have extended back as far as the Hittites who established a royal city called Apasas there.[15] Persistent myth also links the female warriors called Amazons with the founding of the sanctuary of Artemis there, and as the original keepers of the temple that later expanded to become one of the largest in the Hellenistic world. That myth goes on to include martial confrontation with the incoming Ionians and the final defeat and death of the Amazons on the steps of the temple they founded. The graphic possibilities of this myth inevitably attracted artistic interpretation during the Classical period and became the subject of a competition between five famous sculptors of the age, including Praxiteles.[16] The winning entry was a large bronze grouping showing five dying Amazons fighting to protect their beloved Artemis from indignity. While this bronze has not survived, it most certainly must have been quite dramatic, and like 'the Dying Gaul' grouping at Pergamon, it went beyond purely aesthetic interpretations into the realm of a political commentary on the tragic destruction of an indigenous culture by outsiders. Like the Pergamenes, the Ionians realised that they represented a minority in an alien territory, and this sculpture may have represented a sophisticated peace offering.

Like Miletus, Ephesus was also dependent upon its deep harbour for survival, and as at Miletus, this harbour, which penetrated to the edge of its agora, had long since silted up, leaving only a barren plain in its place. Lying in a projected cleft between Mount Pion (Bülbuldag) to the north, and Mount Koressos (Panayirdag) on the south, Ephesus seems more stately, self-controlled and secure than Miletus as it looks out to what was once a frenetic harbour to the west. This same harbour was extremely popular when it was in operation because of its central position along the Aegean coast of

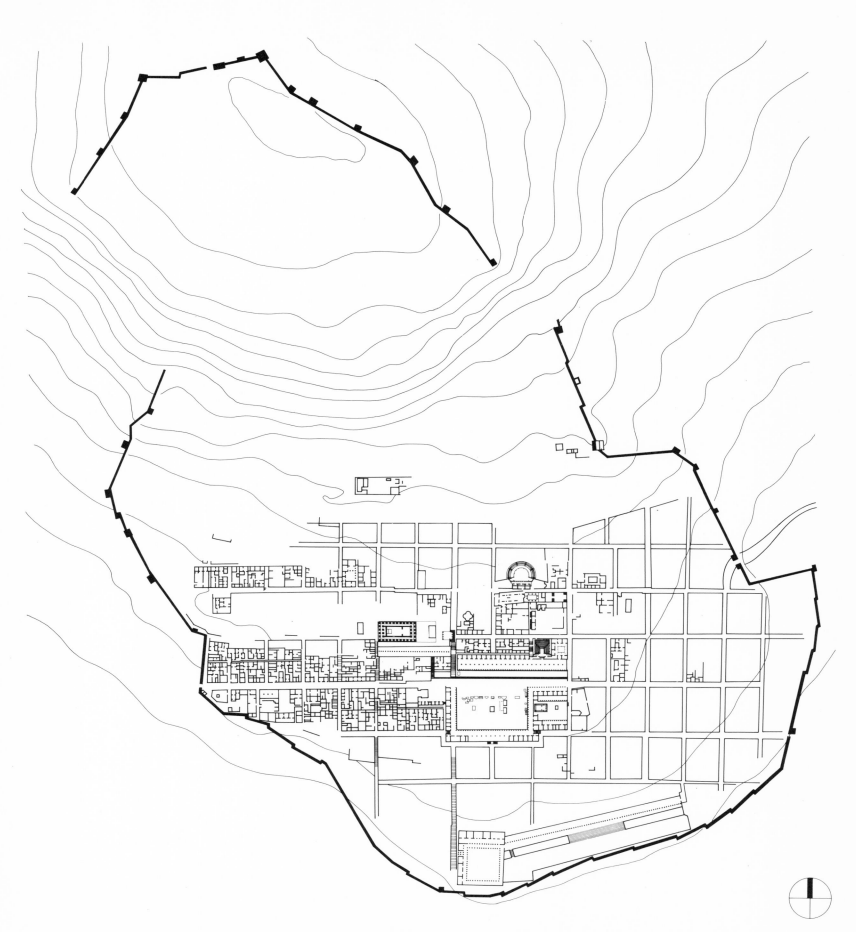

Priene, site plan

Asia Minor, and its convenient location also made pilgrimage to the Artemesion very easy. Rather than facing its harbour with a screen-like, column-lined stoa placed at right angles to it as Miletus did, Ephesus greeted those landing by ship with an enormous gymnasium. While the siting of this particular building may initially seem to have been dictated by a wish to place it as close to the area of highest activity in the city as possible, it also seems to have been selected as a way to show off what was obviously considered to be the most impressive civic monument that Ephesus had to offer. As GMA Hanfmann has said: 'The Greek cities . . . pushed for gymnasia, baths and theatres as major status symbols (and) that type of urban complex . . . was a major creative achievement of Asiatic urbanism . . . With its multiple functions as civic centre, club house, leisure area, school, and place of worship of emperors, the gymnasium now replaced the place and the temple as the major concern of Asiatic cities.'[17] A long stoa running perpendicular to the harbour separated this gymnasium from a broad street bordered by the irregular city wall to the south, leading all pedestrian traffic inexorably towards the famous theatre that still forms the centre of gravity of the town. The ruins of the theatre as seen today date from, the Roman period, as do most other remains still visible there and were the background for the riot against St Paul mentioned in *Acts* that took place around 50 AD led by a craftsman who represented all those involved in making votive statues of the goddess Artemis for sale to tourists.[18] This riot was clearly caused by the fear that many in the city felt about the spread of Christianity and the economic consequences of it.

Priene, which is most memorable for the strict imposition of a Hippodamean grid upon its dramatic cliff-side site, did not share the same symbiotic relationship with its harbour, which was called Naulochos, as Miletus or Ephesus did, but did rely upon it as a lifeline nonetheless. Because of its relatively inaccessible location, much of Priene's formidable circuit wall, as well as many of its public buildings, have remained basically intact and still present a vivid image of the city as it must have been in the Hellenistic period. The fine state of preservation of many buildings such as the bouleuterion to the north of the central agora has greatly improved the contemporary understanding of the function of such buildings. Like Miletus, Priene is a masterpiece of open public spaces that are effectively separated from the private residential areas that surround them and is very instructive of the ways in which a regular grid can become a liberating rather than a restrictive device in urban planning. In the private realm, the courtyard houses that have survived in the western part of the city are also in a good state of preservation, and rival those in both Ephesus and Delos in their ability to recall the everyday life of the people who once lived there. Besides providing a clear example of what Jacqueline Trywhitt once called the 'human-scale intermediary' in urban planning, in which there is a logical graduation of open spaces from public agora to private residential courtyard in the city that never traumatised its inhabitants, both the variety of scale and degree of finish in these homes show how far contemporary expectations of what can be achieved in average domestic surroundings have deteriorated.

Herakleia, which is known as Kapikiri today, and was never officially a part of the pan-Ionian League, lies some distance inland to the east of Miletus and Priene. Taking its Hellenistic name from the god Herakles, the city was originally called Latmos after the mountain on which its acropolis was sited. In spite of its present distance from the Aegean, historians such as Strabo report that the city

Assos, site plan

once had access to the sea and so its alluvian plain, like that now surrounding Troy, dramatically demonstrates just how much the original landscape of the city has changed.[19] Lake Bafa, then, is obviously just a vestigial remnant of that ancient harbour, which is known to have served as a port until the first century BC.[20] The walls that once came down to this harbour's edge still blend perfectly in colour and outline with the boulders that its builders once used as a base, and seem to have magically grown out of them in the past. Unlike the elegantly dressed stone used in the sanctuaries of Endymion or Athena in the market square nearby, this masonry is roughly laid up as befits its more mundane military purpose. A tall watchtower located over five hundred metres above the lake, on the crest of a mountain to the north of the city, is the highest of the sixty-five bastions that were used to punctuate the six-kilometre-long string of wall that was cast around Herakleia, and still serve as a graphic reminder of the uncertainty of the times in which they were built.

Ionia seemed to shine brighter than all of the other regions along the Aegean coast of Asia, providing an inestimable number of famous scholars and artisans to Hellas itself.[21] The combined wealth of all of the cities of the pan-Ionian League inevitably attracted the covetous glances of several neighbouring territories such as those of Lydia with its capital city of Sardis to the east. While Miletus is estimated to have had a population of close to sixty-five thousand around the time of Alexander's invasion of Asia Minor, Sardis was limited to fifty thousand or so within the two hundred and fifty acres that made up its urban area.[22] The river Pactolus, which formed the western-most boundary of the city, once yielded enormous quantities of gold that gave Croesus his legendary reputation as the richest king in history. Gold refineries appear to have been in peak operation between 600 and 550 BC, and considerably enriched what otherwise appear to have been a characteristically bi-nuclear Hellenic city, with an acropolis at its highest point and the remainder of its functions below. Archaeologist GMA Hanfmann, however, has noted an interesting peculiarity that is unique to this city, in that for some mysterious reason it seems to have been partitioned off into distinct zones by high mud brick walls.[23] Aside from the clearly legible remains of the temple of Artemis near the crest of Mount Tmolo, the most complete and impressive ruins at Sardis are those of the massive synagogue that once served a wealthy Jewish community of well in excess of a thousand people.[24] The exquisite beauty and high level of finish of the marble revetments that still remain on this building give eloquent testimony to the high degree of sophistication of the original structure. This community also figured prominently in the Maccabean revolt of the second century AD when the liberal Jews of Sardis requested a gymnasium of their own from King Antiochos IV, and were consequently considered scandalous as a result.[25]

There is strong evidence that the hand of Croesus the builder was at work in Aeolian Assos as well as in Sardis and Ephesus. This small but important coastal city is felt to have come under Lydian control in the sixth century BC, but is best known as one of the formative influences on the great philosopher Aristotle who set up a school there prior to his having been summoned to Pella by Philip of Macedon to take on the responsibility of tutoring the young Alexander. The Hellenistic city once blanketed the steeply sloped south facing hillside on which only the barest traces of its fan-shaped agora and semi-circular theatre now remain. Ironically, as with a great number of the cities that have been mentioned, it is the walls around its perimeter that have survived the best, providing a dramatic contrast to the more ephemeral civil amenities. The agora itself, which is commonly illustrated in history texts as being located on a flat site, is actually only a brief respite from a cliff-like slope that closely rivals that at Priene. This cliff rises abruptly from the harbour at its base, where the marble quay where Aristotle possibly once lectured is still visible beneath the turquoise water, to the crest of the acropolis two hundred and thirty-five metres above. The ruins of the temple that once dominated this acropolis now lie completely strewn around its base, but it is still possible to note that it was of the Doric order, which is extremely rare in this region. Vincent Scully has logically proposed that the reason for this surprising variation from local tradition may have been that the temple, although relatively small in scale, seemed so imposing when seen from the agora that the more intricate Ionic order typically used elsewhere would have been too visually disturbing when seen by those below.[26] The peristyle of this temple, which had thirteen columns on each side and six on the ends, enclosed only a small narrow cella in its centre. A relatively complete mosaic that dates from the Hellenistic period still remained intact until very recently, but has now vanished. The area of the agora below was quite large, one hundred and fifty by sixty metres at its longest, east-west axis, which worked with the slope and placed its major south facing elevation towards the sea. A large two-storey-high stoa on the opposite, northern side, created a barrier against the steep slope beside it. A square bouleuterion anchored the compressed, eastern end of the fan-shaped complex, which opened up slightly on the west to showcase a small prostyle temple. In spite of the poor state of preservation of the major civic buildings in the city, Assos continues to hold a special fascination that few of the other sites in Asia Minor do, possibly because of the more comprehensible human scale of the entire complex.

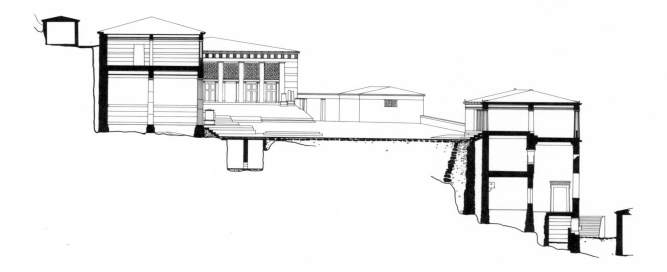

Section through agora looking towards the bouleuterion, Assos

49

Side, site plan

THE INSTITUTIONS

When Alexander the Great entered Asia Minor, he found the land there to be divided in three ways: between the Persian king, the cities, and the temples themselves.[1] The king's land, which made up the major portion of the area, typically included such things as mineral resources and forests that could provide revenue for the king, as well as large properties that had been given over to those with whom the crown had found favour. This privileged aristocracy continued to maintain their land in a feudal relationship with the king, and also paid taxes to him. The occupants of the cities and villages were serfs in most cases, farming the surrounding agricultural areas, and also paying taxes to the king. In instances where a city had been begun by Greek colonists in the past and had been granted the status of *katoikoi*, or of having free hereditary settlers; the city was often released from the condition of serfdom.[2] Temple estates, however, were one of the most novel institutions to confront Alexander and his army; and also occupied a large portion of the land in Asia Minor. These were socio-religious foundations with a long tradition that predated any of the Persian or Greek temples there, and were based on the older matriarchal cults of Anatolia. These estates normally grew up around recognised centres of worship and were administered by the high priest or priestess of a particular fertility goddess. They operated in a time-honoured system that condoned the priestly control of an enormous amount of land surrounding the temple, and the collection of taxes from the local people who worked that land. The young daughters of these people were routinely expected to serve as prostitutes in the temple prior to their marriage in order to assist in the worship of the fertility goddess and to provide an earthly example of the basic aspect of her character. Because of the significant amount of revenue collected through farm revenues, taxation and prostitution, the temple itself also gradually assumed the role of a bank for the area around it, and kept this function well into the Hellenistic Age. Records kept by these temple estates indicate that great numbers of people served them. The temple of 'The place of the hymns', or Ma of Comana, in Cappadocia, for example, is known to have had over six thousand temple slaves, and the estate of Men Askaenos, near Antioch in Pisidia probably had far more.[3] In contrast to Alexander's *laissez-faire* attitude towards the estates, the general policy of the Successors was to reduce them, and to convert that portion of the land that was not absolutely necessary for the sustenance of the temple itself into kings' land. Even these vastly reduced religious reservations did not remain entirely sacrosanct however, as wars increased the need for revenue and temple treasuries were violated with more and more frequency.

The grafting of the Greek religious pantheon onto these existing Anatolian cults produced some interesting anomalies, such as the Temple of Artemis at Ephesus. Prior to its conversion into one of the seven wonders of the ancient world by the Greeks, the site of this temple had been sacred to the

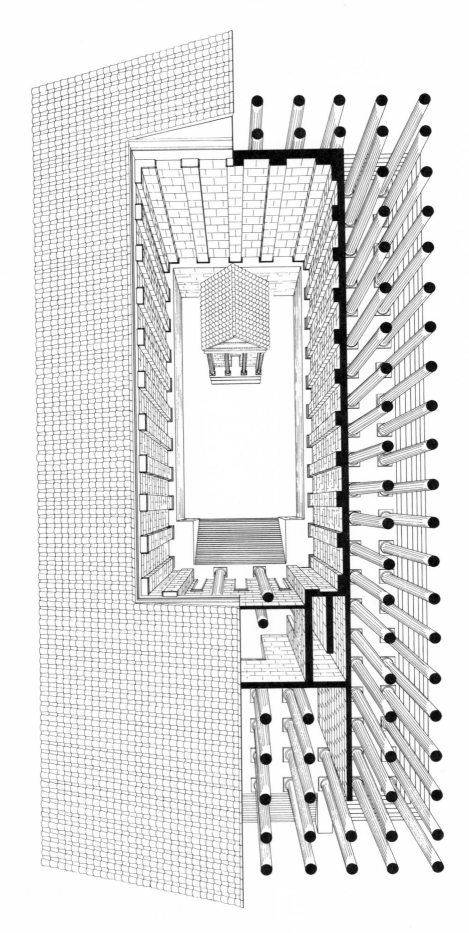

Cut-away plan perspective, Temple of Apollo, Didyma

Anatolian goddess Cybele, whose priests modelled their organisation on the social structure of bees.[4] This community was ruled by the Mega-Byzas, or King Bee, who presided over numerous temple assistants. Artemis herself was a metamorphosis of the goddess Cybele and was considered to have the same powers over the natural world that had once been granted to her predecessor. The statues of Artemis-Cybele that have survived still retain the exaggerated anatomical features of the prehistoric mother goddess also known as Kubala, Hepa or Lat in previous manifestations. As a continuing reminder that she was the queen of the beasts, the Hellenised version of the goddess still retained vivid reminders of her former role, such as a skirt made up of the heads of the animals whom she was thought to protect, and a multitude of grape-like clusters of breasts. The entire aspect of the goddess, as represented in the statues of the Hellenistic period, is unmistakably Eastern, from the addition of these strikingly naturalistic features to her flat-topped, pill-box crown.

The Temple of Apollo at Didyma, near Miletus, offers another good example of the mixing of Mediterranean and oriental sensibilities that took place at this time and provides a study of the Hellenistic attitude towards religion in microcosm. At Didyma the temple is not only to be appreciated as a sculptural object set in its unique landscape, as in the past, but is rather, a temple within a temple in which an ideal inner world is created. The perfection sought in the highly symbolic interior zone of the building seems to present an intentionally idyllic alternative to the politically unstable climate that existed outside the walls of the sanctuary. To achieve this protective enclave, the scale of the outer shell of the temple was increased far beyond normal standards. With a stylobate measuring 109.34 metres by 51.13 metres, the temple was the third largest in the Hellenistic world, following the Artemision at Ephesus and the Temple of Hera at Samos.[5]

Within this initial perimeter a man-made forest of breathtakingly slender Ionic columns is used to screen a massive cella that is totally open to the sky. Inside this cliff-like enclosure, or *naiskos*, there was a smaller, second temple that represented the home of Apollo. This faced the sacred oracular spring through which he was thought to speak. The entire ground surface was planted with symmetrical rows of laurel trees, which were also associated with the god. Just as the Athenian Parthenon played an important part in the celebrations of a city paying homage to its own unity, the Didymaon of Apollo was also the final goal of a pilgrimage road that led to it from Miletus, which exercised titular control over it. In a much more profound way than the Parthenon, however, the Didyma temple also represents an individual, rather than collective journey and diagrams, in a highly symbolic way, all of the frustrations and delights encountered by a single soul. The petrified version of the natural world that is constructed within the naiskos is the architectural translation of a paradise, and sequence, scale and symbolism are used to tell the story of its attainment. As in the Egyptian temple, that sequence is also linear and progressively more meaningful. After climbing a 3.5-metres-high *krepidoma* lined with seven wide steps, the worshipper penetrates through five densely spaced rows of high columns to find the door into the cella itself. Rather than a framed opening of the normal kind, however, the central door is here blocked by a ledge, or stage, that is raised about one and a half metres above the ground to act effectively as a barrier to further progress. This was the *chresmographeion*, where the priests announced the oracles of Apollo to those waiting below. As a high, compact and rectilinear room in its own right, the chresmographeion had a roof that was supported by two massive interior columns, and a long stairway on its inaccessible inner wall that the priests used to gain access to it from the sacred naiskos. Standing at the foot of the chresmographeion, the worshipper could not see further into the naiskos itself, but did have an angular view upwards through the room to the sky that was visible through the open cella. The intentional contrast between the dark and dappled shade of the thickly columned pronaos and bright blue sky seen through the slotted back wall of the chresmographeion not only reinforced the metaphor of passage that was beginning to be played out, but also encouraged the worshipper to overcome this initial barrier and search further for a way into the interior. This was made possible through a set of ramps and stairs that flank the chresmographeion, which each have entrances that are not initially obvious. These both lead down to the sacred court, which is at the same level as the ground-plane exterior. The scene presented to the worshipper after having descended through one of the long, dark tunnels was one of Elysian perfection and purity, that, according to Vincent Scully, was 'calculated to set up a baroque drama of basic sensations in the mind of the observer. The emotions so aroused must have made the complex nature of Apollo almost fully comprehensible; shelter and coolness in his grove, the taste of death in the dark restriction of his caves, release from the darkness once again into the trapped sunlight of the court with its whispering leaves.'[6]

This drama was heightened by the climactic view of the Temple of Apollo itself, seen primarily in elevation at the opposite end of the long, rectilinear courtyard through rows of laurel trees.

A dado, which was set into the wall of the cella to establish a datum between the level of the chresmographeion and that of the court, inevitably led the eye of those at the entrance to this small architectural gem, that was built in the Ionian order and was made to appear to rise vertically because of the towering Corinthian pilasters that held up the sheer, twenty-five-metre-high walls of the cella that surrounded it. The vegetal capitals that crowned the tops of these tree-like shafts blended perfectly with a similarly executed band that ran between them. This entire line of abstracted greenery, in turn, tended to soften the hard edge of the canyon rim framing the blue sky above, and provided a lofty parallel to the lushness of the laurel trees in the courtyard below.

The calculated effects that were so central to the impact of the Didymaon show the extent to which the entire concept of the temple had changed, as well as the profound revisions that exposure to the cultures of the East had introduced. Initially conceived as the supernatural equivalent of the temporal palace, the temple was at first only slightly altered to adapt to its specific site, and the two together were meant to reflect the particular characteristics of the deity to whom they were dedicated. As the members of the Olympic pantheon, Zeus, Hera, Athena, Apollo, Artemis, Poseidon, Aphrodite, Hermes, Hesphaestus, Ares, Demeter and Dionysus were each visualised as the embodiment of a specific natural phenomenon that could best be expressed through the interaction of temple and landscape.[7] From the beginning the Greek temple was a trabeated, column and beam structure that retained this system of construction not out of ignorance about the arch, but in the belief that trabeation offered a much more effective visual linkage between the man made and the natural. By presenting a repetitive series of horizontal and vertical structural members as a frame to the distant landscape that was seen through them, the trabeated system most closely matched the Greek sensibilities about the dualities that were implicit in the very idea of man trying to build a house for a deity in a natural setting.[8] While a concerted effort was made to join the temple and its surroundings into one architectural statement, there was always the underlying realisation that as a construct of man in nature they could never really join; just as humans and gods, who shared many similar attributes, could never share immortality. The slow evolution of the temple form, from a simple wooden shelter to a precision-crafted marble replica of this primary structure, offers an unparalleled example of the incremental perfection of an architectural idea. Rather than being the single expression of an individual ego, this building type became the physical translation of a collective cultural consciousness that was gradually refined over time. Wide deviations from that consciousness, rather than being encouraged, were instead considered to be a break of the collective will, and those involved in the design of the temple sought creative expression within the norms that had already been established.

A convenient explanation for the erosion of this collective consciousness in the Hellenistic Age would obviously seem to be the influence of the exotic cultures that then began to blend into one. The social causes behind the gradual weakening in the belief in the traditional pantheon, however, were far more complex, and were actually based on the growing concern about personal security in the midst of the escalating violence of the wars of the Successors; and the inadequacy of pantheism in dealing with the almost constant prospect of a brutal death. The results of these wars, in addition to that of the earlier Peloponnesian War, also seemed to reinforce the fact that good men, representing the cause of justice, almost always seemed to lose out to those of less noble character. The rise of one ruler and the fall of others seemed to be totally arbitrary, and completely unrelated to either religious devotion or morality. Men with high values and relatively altruistic motives, such as Eumenes, or Seleucus, did have some initial success, but eventually were superseded by others, like Cassander, or Ptolemy, who did not. The apparent randomness involved in political fortunes began to undermine the basic Greek belief in the concept of *dike*, which rather than translating simply as 'justice', had more to do with an amoral, dispassionate order of things related to a natural course of events that had an intrinsic direction of their own. That direction, however, was always felt to favour good over evil.[9]

The role of Zeus as the embodiment of *dike*, and the 'guide of fate', or *moiragetes*, began to be replaced by that of *tyche*, or fortune, and the belief that each human life was irrevocably fixed into a certain pattern prior to birth.[10] This concept was reinforced by the new philosophical theories that were then gaining prominence, such as those of the Stoics who were promoting the idea of courageous acceptance of immutable fate and 'the allotted portion of man', or *heimarmene moira*.[11] These views were also supported by the rationalistic ideas of Aristotle. The renewed study of astrological charts that was then taking place in Seleucid Babylon dovetailed nicely with this shift towards a belief in *tyche*, and teachers from as far away as Uruk began to appear in the Aegean. Records discovered at Kos, for example, note a visit by an astrologer called Berossus the Babylonian, in the Hellenistic period, indicating a heightened interest in that subject there.[12]

While oracles such as those at Delphi, Delos, and Didyma had always been considered to be an acceptable adjunct to the function of the temple, their popularity greatly increased at this time because of the rush to believe in anything that could offer some degree of stability amidst so much change. There is also evidence of a search for new gods, or *theoi epekooi*, who would listen to prayer, to replace those of the past who did not.[13] This change in attitude was also responsible for a hyphenating trend, that attempted to find gods with similar attributes from various cultures and to link them together in the hope that prayers to them would then be more effective. As a result of this trend, traditional Greek gods such as Zeus, who was once believed to be he head of the Olympic Pantheon, were joined with Amon of Egypt as were Hadad and Ahuramazda of Mesopotamia, and Aphrodite with Hathor and Astarte, to name just a few.

One of the most noticeable results of all of these changes was a gradual shift away from the intuitive, visceral and pantheistic relationship between man and nature that had previously existed, to a more formal and detached attitude towards religion. Because of this detachment and the constant disruptions of civic life, caused by war and by the synoecism, or joining of one city to another in Asia Minor for administrative convenience, the traditional relationship between the polis and a particular god or goddess was weakened and in many cases became meaningless. The increased commercialisation of the temple was another symptom of this greater formality, as can be inferred from the dramatic rise in the scale of the sacrificial offerings that were made, as well as the priestly offices and votive objects that were sold.[14] While it would be tempting to begin to trace the new trend towards larger sacrifices to the example set by Alexander's mother Olympias, who was never one to be known for her religious restraint and self-control, there are many earlier cases of excess. The extensive use of sacrificial animals had long been common in the religious ceremonies of Mesopotamia, as can be seen by a cuneiform tablet from Uruk that lists fifty rams, two bulls, one ox and eight lambs as the daily sacrifice made there. King Croesus of Sardis also once sacrificed three thousand animals at a single ceremony at the Temple of Delphi, and Seleucus contributed one thousand sheep and a dozen bulls to the oracle at Didyma.[15] The infamous Greek altar of Pergamon, which St John refers to as 'the Throne of Satan' in the biblical book of *Revelations*, was obviously designed to deal with sacrifices on a grand scale in addition to effectively serving a political purpose. This altar, which has now been partially reconstructed inside the Pergamon Museum in Berlin, completely occupied centre stage on a terrace of its own that was wedged between the Pergamene agora below it and the Athena temple and library directly above. Unfortunately, only faint traces of the foundation of this enormous structure still remain visible on the site today, and give just a slight hint of the visual impact it must have had. The altar, which was jointly dedicated to Zeus and Athena, was built during the reign of Eumenes II to celebrate his victory over the Gauls in 190 BC, and it is their valour and bravery in defeat that is allegorically immortalised in the frieze showing a battle between gods and giants that animates its base. In spite of the fact that it is located on a terrace that is twenty-five metres lower than that of the Athena Temple and library next to it, which was built nearly a century earlier, the desire to give the city an impressive, formal face prompted its builders to bring the imposing western side of the altar into exact alignment with that of the temple above.[16] The entrance to the altar, however, was organised through a ceremonial gateway on its opposite, eastern side, making it necessary for those approaching to circle around one side of the building in order to reach the monumental staircase leading up to the sacrificial table in the interior. This circuitous approach, which tended to make the altar seem even larger than it was by presenting a higher and more imposing side to the procession as it moved through the entrance gate, also prolonged the beginning of the sacrifice itself. By doing so, a ceremony that had by this time become somewhat routine was made to be far more exciting.[17] In a variation on the theme of the titanic struggle that was sculpturally depicted elsewhere, the frieze on this entrance side, which faced the sunrise, showed Zeus and Athena in relief, as well as Apollo, Artemis and Leto, who were the gods and goddesses associated with light. The massive rectilinear sacrificial table used for blood offerings, however, which was more than fifteen-metres long and five-metres wide, was far from luminous, and greatly exceeded the size of any other that then existed. As the frequently stained counterpoint to the abstract perfection of the temple, the sacrificial table was, as Walter Burkett has described it, where 'the worshipper experiences the god most powerfully not just in pious conduct or in prayer, song, and dance, but in the deadly blow of the axe, the gush of blood and the burning of thigh pieces.'[18] The sequence followed in this sacrifice had been established by long tradition, starting with bathing, putting on clean clothes and the sexual abstinence imperative for Muslims prior to the sacrifice which is still required at the end of the Hadj today. This cleansing is followed by the procession, which was led by a virgin carrying a basket, and was accompanied by music and singing. This movement from the profane world to the sacred realm of the altar was reinforced upon arrival at the final destination, as the basket containing the knife that would be used to kill the sacrificial animal was carried in front of the circle of people that formed around the altar. After each one had washed their hands from a common water jug, and the sacrificial animal itself had been washed, barley grains were thrown towards it as a symbolic act of aggression prior to the death blow being struck. When the fatal knife-cut was finally made, the women gave a 'sacrificial scream', or *ololyge*, that heightened the terror of the moment and covered any sound that the animal itself might have made.[19] Great attention was then paid to make sure that all of the life-giving blood washed the altar and was not defiled in falling to the ground, before the animal was butchered, and the pieces distributed according to custom.

The central dichotomy involved in this ritual that ensured its survival for thousands of years was that through the act of killing in such a controlled way, the value of life, and especially communal life, was reaffirmed. As in any ritual, the original intention behind many of the actions that were carried out had long been forgotten, but the social need to continue them remained, and therefore the ritual or sacrifice was perpetuated. Ritual itself has been defined as 'a behaviour pattern that has lost its primary function . . . but which persists in a new function, that of communication . . . This communicating function reveals the two basic characteristics of ritual behaviour, namely, repetition and theatrical exaggeration.'[20]

Such theatrical exaggeration has been identified as one of the original motivations behind the creation of the institution of the theatre in Ionian Anatolia, where it is felt to have begun primarily in the formalisation of burial, rather than sacrificial rites.[21] The derivation of the word 'theatre' comes from the Greek word *theatron* or 'a place of seeing' which strongly reinforces the possibility of ritualistic origins as does the circular orchestra or 'dancing place' that characterises the most archaic examples of the type.[22] The possible connection of the god Dionysus with such dancing and the presence of sacrificial altars in the middle of many of the earliest orchestra circles, however, raises questions about its having first been exclusively used for burial ceremonies, and all that can be said with any certainty, is that group dancing in a flat, circular area in the presence of spectators was the beginning of the theatre. The chorus, which formed a major part of many of the Classical plays that have survived, is a convincing vestige of these choreographic beginnings, as is the obvious musical structure and character of the works themselves. In its evolution through the politically and religiously significant tragedies of Aeschylus, Sophocles and Euripides through to the new comedy, the changes that take place in Greek drama substantially mirror those affecting the society itself. The development of the new comedy in Athens in the hands of playwrights like Menander, whose dates of 342 to 292 BC spanned the period of both Alexander and the Successors, unquestionably altered the traditional, theatrical forms of the past. The world Menander describes in his plays is one in which order is nostalgically sought within a private and individual world, since it was no longer possible to expect any degree of security in the public realm. In a fascinating parallel to Post-Modern literature a similar sense of powerlessness seems to pervade this work, and also seems to convey a longing for a reversion into the past. There is also a deep sense of belief in the prevalence of random chance over calculated and rational action as well as a growing impression of the limited ability of the individual to cope with the increasingly complicated political machinations of the times. Menander's pat prescription is a retreat into the certain security of the family group as well as the private world of the intellect.

The immediately recognisable physical impact of the new comedy, in its emphasis of such highly-individualised characterisation, was the emergence of the proscenium stage, which was a major change in theatre design. In conjunction with this new raised and projecting platform from which the actors could be seen more easily, it also became possible to hang elaborately painted backdrops from the extended arcades on which the proscenium was supported. While these arcades provided an excellent opportunity to present scenes of exotic locations in a three-dimensional way, the actual effect of the raised stage was the blocking of the immediate view of the natural world close at hand, and the subsequent divorce of the theatre from it. The hermetically sealed, artificial view that was created, and that continued to evolve in the Roman theatre, was alleviated somewhat by locating the seating area on a steep slope, so that sweeping, panoramic views of the surrounding landscape were still possible over the top of the stage as can be seen in Priene, Pergamon and Ephesus.

The ubiquity of the theatre as a constantly recurring element in all of the Hellenised cities in Asia Minor, and its importance as a civic symbol among those striving to be so, is matched only by that of the gymnasium, which seems to have had an uncanny ability of survival over and above all other building types. The gymnasium began to transcend its earlier purpose as a place for military training when elevated to the level of a symbol of Greek culture by Alexander in his establishment of cities throughout the East. As such, it was recognised by the historian Pausanias as one of the requisite elements for a city to be worthy of its name. 'The place of nakedness', the gymnasium, forced the more inhibited members of the indigenous societies which the Greeks proselytised literally to strip away any of the reservations they may have had about the strange habits of the foreigners in their midst in order to belong to this very select club. From the beginning however, the gymnasium continued to fulfil its complex function as a combination between an athletic centre, school of philosophy and music and social meeting place. The reason behind this seemingly incompatible mixture of activities was the formative Greek belief in *paideia*, or the need to achieve the ideal balance between mental and physical perfection within the human body.[23] The gymnasium component related to physical well-being had originally been a separate entity called the palaestra where largely individual sports such as track, discus and javelin throwing and wrestling were practised.[24]

While remaining separate in several circumstances, the palaestra unit was gradually subsumed into the form of the gymnasium as time went by. Educationally, the gymnasium divided its activities between both younger and older students and focused its attentions on adolescents, called *ephebes*. At Pergamon, for example, this division is physically expressed in the stepped, tripartite arrangement of the gymnasium on the slope, where each section is placed according to the rank and age of its members and called *neos*, *ephebos* and *pais* in their turn.[25] While much of the lower gymnasium at the base of the hillside has disappeared, the names of many of the children who began their training there have been inscribed on the walls for posterity. The middle gymnasium or ephebos, on the terrace above it shares its flat terrace with a temple of Herakles, who was one of the gods associated with sport, on its eastern end, which makes a clear statement about the close connection between religion and higher educational endeavour in this society. The ephebion holds pride of place among all three levels and symmetrically dominates the central axis that runs through all of them. The bilateral formality of this zone is indirectly in keeping with the ceremonial nature of many of the activities that took place here such as the awarding of prizes, and graduation to the status of full citizenship. Three levels of ephebes are known to have been recognised in this school, and membership was granted not only to sons of citizens of the city, but also to boys from local villages under its direct control as well as sons of distinguished visitors.[26] The elaborate sequence of baths that became such an integral part of hygienic rituals in the Roman period, were not viewed in the same way in the early stages of the gymnasium. Rather than washing prior to exercise, the Greeks oiled their bodies in an *elaisthesium*, or oiling room, and then washed briskly and sequentially in the fairly shallow pool of a hot bath, or *cauldarium* which opened the pores and cleaned them, prior a final plunge in the *frigidarium* to cool down, and a vigorous scraping to remove water, oil and dirt from the skin. The introduction of the *tepidarium* in the midst of this sequence began to encourage long, lolling social soaks at the baths for extended periods of time, and seems to have been a late Hellenistic and Roman innovation. When transplanted into the cities of the East in the Hellenistic Age, the gymnasium could no longer remain the exclusive enclave that it had been in the past and came under increasing pressure to lower the standards of admission. At its best, in locations as far flung as Lycian Termessos, or Aikhanoun, Afghanistan, it brilliantly served its purpose as a highly visible repository of the highest philosophical and physical ideals of Hellenic culture, and provided an unmistakable, if somewhat isolated model of these ideals for all to see.

Pausanias' characterisation of the institutions necessary to make up a city, as mentioned earlier were more succinctly stated as: 'No gymnasium, no theatre, no water supply, no city'.[28] The remarkable consistency of these institutions throughout all of the diverse regions of Anatolia, shows the extent to which Alexander succeeded in his conversion efforts. The architectural legacy of that effort still remains as a testament to the diversity that is possible by working within the accepted order of culturally proscribed tradition.

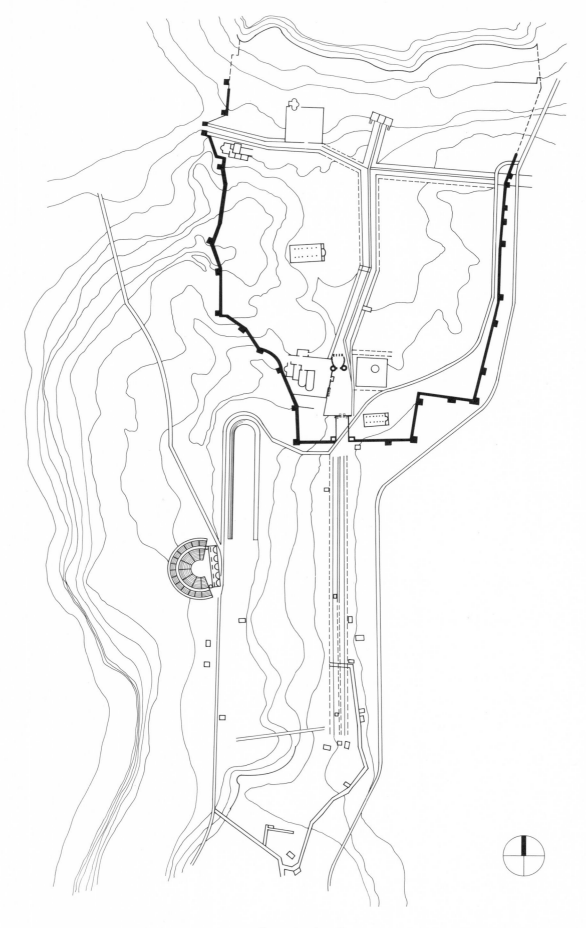

Perge, site plan

THE HELLENISTIC
LEGACY

In most contemporary studies of Ancient Greece, the Hellenistic period is frequently characterised as the illegitimate step-child of a far more significant Classical Age, or is, at best, treated as a time during which each of the far-flung fragments of the empire that Alexander had left behind sought to consolidate the endangered values of the past. One such study, which may be considered typical of this opinion, states that:

> The great creative period, at least with respect to those elements of Greek Civilisation which mattered most, had come to an end in Alexander's day. There were later exceptions but the four hundred or so years between Homer and Aristotle produced nearly all the key ideas, literature and art forms that were transmitted to later ages and centuries.[1]

In order to assess the historical influence of both the Classical and Hellenistic periods at least in an architectural sense, it may be helpful to trace briefly the basic means of that transmission so that the validity of such claims can be more accurately determined. While there may be some debate about the degree of influence that various periods of Ancient Greek architecture have had upon the successive waves of Neo-Classicism that seem to have taken place with surprising regularity over the last four centuries there can be little argument that the medium for what has been called a 'Classical transition' was Roman architecture.[2] Lacking any substantial tectonic tradition of its own at the beginning of its meteoric rise to power, Rome initially relied heavily upon Etruscan artisans for the designs and construction of their temples and other public buildings.[3] As Varro said, in his *Lingua Latina*: 'The Romans initiated the Etruscan style in architecture.'[4] By an accident of history, the Etruscans, in turn, had been relatively insulated from the zenith of Classical influence that surrounded them, passing, as has been noted, almost directly from an archaic phase of development into the late Hellenistic mannerisms of the fourth and third centuries.[5] This initial Roman exposure by Etruscan guidance, to Hellenistic instead of High-Classical influence was further augmented and paralleled by continuous martial expansion during the Pyrrhic and Samnite wars carried out in southern Italy in the fourth century BC. During the last half of the third century this was followed, as JMC Toynbee has said, by widespread pillaging by victorious Roman generals such as Marcellus in 212 BC which 'marked the beginning of the mass importation into Rome of the art treasures of the Hellenistic world. In the second century this process was extended eastwards across the Adriatic to Greece proper and Asia Minor.'[6] This progressively increasing degree of influence from Eastern, rather than Latin sources can now be traced in many historical writings of that time, such as those of Livy, who described what he considered to be the disintegration of the simplicity of the traditional Roman way of life by saying in 187 BC that 'the beginnings of foreign luxury were introduced into the city by the army from Asia'.[7] In Book VI of his work on architecture Vitruvius also makes reference to what he called *consuetudo italica* or the Hellenistic style, which Roman builders could not resist, as well as going on to recount in Book VII that the rebuilding of the Olympicion in Athens in 175 BC was commissioned by none other than the Seleucid King, Antiochos IV, who used a Roman named Decimus Cossutius as the builder.[8] This strong influence from the East, and most especially from Asia Minor, pervaded every aspect of Roman life even transforming building types as sacrosanct as the temple itself; which symbolised not only continuity with the past, but also the growing cults of imperial authority. As Axel Boethus has said:

> The Romans were more original in other fields of architecture but a survey of the late Republican temples gives us the best notion of the traditionalistic Hellenism in the centuries from Naevius and Ennius to Cicero and the young Virgil. The theatre-temples show us how the fundamental Etruscan and Italic traditions could become almost effaced by the variegated combinations and decorations of Hellenistic architecture.[9]

Such architectural transformations were only surface indications of deeper social changes such as the increasing popularity of the mystery cults that were first encountered in Egypt, Asia Minor, Syria and Babylon by soldiers and traders, as well as those brought back from those areas in captivity.[10] Christianity, as the most successful of all of these, also proved to be the most effective vehicle for the continued transmission of the Hellenistic forms that were then embodied in Roman architecture. With the military vulnerability of Rome itself becoming more apparent in the fourth century AD, and the transposition of the heart of the Empire to Byzantium by Constantine in 325, the lineage of these forms ironically came around in a full circle, and from that point forwards continued to evolve within the closed capsule of Constantinople for another millenium. The decision to move the capital was not made lightly, but was the final result of the Emperor's long political involvement in this part of the world during the reign of Diocletian, when Constantine had held a governmental post in Nicomedia and had overseen an extensive building programme there. The new Rome that Constantine envisioned was not simply to be a poor imitation of its Western counterpart, however, but an improved reproduction, even down to the re-creation of the seven hills and fourteen regions of the original. Thousands of sculptures and other works of art were either commissioned or imported to glorify the new city which used the earlier plan of Septimus Severus as its base. This plan incorporated many temples, as well as baths and a hippodrome, which was to become an important social institution in the new city. The additions that Constantine made to this plan are very instructive of his long range intentions for both the character of his new Rome, and the role that he wished the city to play as the centre of a new empire. The first official act that the Emperor performed was to alter the tertiary relationships between temple, circus and bath that he had inherited from his predecessor by recognising Christianity, and ordering the construction of two churches that he named Holy Wisdom and Holy Peace. By doing so, Constantine sent out a clear message that he wanted his new Rome to be the heart of a Christian empire, rather than a pantheistic one, as the old Rome had been. To extend his personal commitment to this idea even further, he physically linked his own palace directly to the twin churches that he had commissioned, setting up what he felt to be the ideal combination of palace, church and stadium. Almost no trace of the great palace that he built now remains, but those that do suggest that it was probably very similar to the palace that Diocletian built

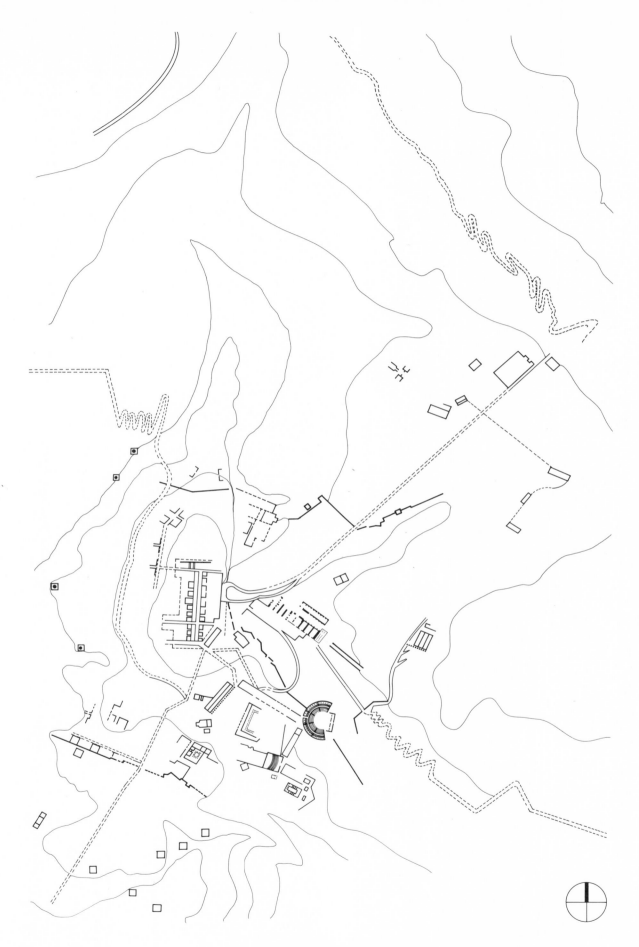

Termessos, site plan

at Split (Spalato), now in Yugoslavia. By inserting his palace into the old, reciprocal relationship between institutions identified with religion and recreation, Constantine physically and symbolically positioned himself as an arbitrator between the church and his subjects. He considered himself to be the thirteenth apostle who was appointed by God to use his authority to expand the mission of Christianity on earth. His vision of himself as the leader of both Church and State is also reflected in the design of the Hagia Sophia that later emerged under Justinian, with its large, circular, central dome, under which the Emperor and Patriarch would meet at the culmination of the worship service. A long line of Byzantine emperors followed Constantine in a continuous one thousand, two-hundred year succession, broken only by the treachery of Doge Dandelo. All considered themselves to be the rightful heirs to a Classical tradition that had been saved from extinction by the fall of Rome. After the first capitulation of Constantinople to crusaders in 1203, and the second fall of the city in 1453 to the Turks under Mehmet the Conqueror, conventional wisdom holds that its scholars headed west, contributing in no small way to the growing intellectual atmosphere that ultimately led to the Renaissance in the late fifteenth and early sixteenth centuries. The mathematical astrological and scientific tradition that those scholars carried with them, as well as the experimental attitude which characterised many of the architects and artisans among them, can now be recognised as having a Hellenistic, rather than a purely Classical basis. The master builders of the Middle Ages in Europe were the direct intellectual descendants of 'geometers' such as Anthemius of Tralles and Isidorus of Miletus.

While the basis of their carefully guarded mathematical secrets were Pythagorean irrational numbers, as well as the 'golden section', and therefore predated Pericles and the Parthenon by a full century, such techniques were also overlayed with Archimedian physics as well as Babylonian and Egyptian mathematical concepts that gave the masonic fraternity of the Middle Ages a distinctly Hellenistic basis.[12] As to the transference of the Medieval reliance on such ratios into the Renaissance AA Armstrong has said that:

> There is every reason to suppose that the architectural mathematics of the Middle Ages were far closer to those of Greece and Rome than those of Renaissance Italy; in fact that there was a straight line of descent — a continuous tradition which ironically was to some extent disrupted by the very zealots who thought they were restoring it.[13]

The Roman architect Vitruvius once again played a major role in the establishment of those mathematics by expanding the concept of geometry to include a knowledge of astronomy, philosophy and science, clearly reflecting the universal attitude of the age that had preceded his own. In Book VII of his *Ten Books on Architecture*, Vitruvius lists twenty-four Classical, as well as, Hellenistic sources in nearly equal numbers, including Pytheos and Hermogenes, who worked in Asia Minor in the fourth and second centuries, respectively.[14]

Incidentally, Robert Adam, who played a central role in the Neo-Classical revival in Britain in the eighteenth century, has further confirmed the persistence and depth of Hellenistic influence upon that period by his own constant reference to Vitruvius in his spectacular study of the ruins of the Palace of Diocletian at Split.[15] As well as the obvious impact that many of the details that he recorded at Split had upon his own work, there is the additional factor of Adam's own ability to inspire imitators in that, and subsequent revivals.[16] The irony of Adam's pivotal role comes not only from the fact that he was inspired by the mentor of the Palace of Constantine, and thereby brought the Western Hellenistic tradition back, in a full circle, to its Eastern source once again, but also from the coincidence of his point of departure. Like Doge Dandelo, who led the crusade that destroyed Constantinople in 1203, Adam also set sail from Venice in 1757 but instead of being motivated by a desire for destruction and pillage, his sole purpose was to gain first-hand knowledge of Classical architecture.

If the stylistic tradition that Adam recorded so exquisitely at Split has had a more pervasive and durable influence than the Classicism that he initially set out to find; because of its transmission through both Roman secular and religious architecture, as well as by the Church and Byzantium; where are its major monuments? Where, it may be asked, is the Hellenistic equivalent of the Parthenon? As the photographs and drawings that have been included here have shown, it would be difficult to isolate one such ultimate example for this period, because of the great variety of choices that exist, but the decision on the location of this example should cause no debate. As noted Hellenistic scholar Christine Havelock has said, it would undoubtedly be: 'In Asia Minor', because 'after the fifth century, after the decline of Athens as a major power, the creative and exciting developments of temple architecture occur not in the Doric but in the Ionic order, and not primarily on the mainland of Greece but in those cities of the East newly founded or conquered by Alexander and his Successors.'[17] Various historical brackets are frequently used to define the Classical Age, including the Persian defeat at Salamis as a beginning, and the battle of Chaeronia as an end. More generally, those brackets are extended to include the four centuries that separate Homer and Aristotle, and the Periclean period between 462 and 429 BC. The Parthenon that it produced, is widely acknowledged to be the most perfect architectural expression of that age. Many have tried to describe just why this is so, typically mentioning precision, workmanship, proportion, balance, tension, perspective corrections that make the temple and its ensemble seem to come alive and assure the position of the Parthenon as the ultimate example of the Doric order. Once again, however, AH Armstrong opens up a perceptive variation on this theme by mentioning that 'in their several ways, the great buildings which came to adorn the Acropolis during the second half of the fifth century broke decisively with precedent . . . one senses a new aesthetic purpose, a different kind of appeal to the imagination than formal symmetry alone could make'.[18] While the Parthenon continued to express the traditional ideal of the habitation of a god or goddess that had evolved out of the Royal Mycenean megaron, with religious celebrations and sacrifices taking place outside rather than in it, the processional nature of the Panathenaia played a critical role in the placement of each element upon the hill, affecting massing, sight angles, column numbers and spacing, colour and decoration, to the most minute detail and extent. When considered from this point of view, the Propylaea, Temple of Athena Nike, Erechtheon and Parthenon transcend a purely religious function, becoming the architectural embodiment of the combined political will and aspirations of Athens. The Acropolis, then, was not only the home of the goddess who was the deified totem of the city, but also became the symbol of the extended imperial identity of Athens.

At its zenith, this empire also included all of the cities in the old Ionian League of Asia Minor which

Xanthos, site plan

had reason to depend on Athens for protection from the Persian menace nearby. This link was not only financially beneficial for Athens, but also had a genealogical basis, since the legends of many of the members in that league included the name of the Athenian King Codrus as being a semi-mythical founder. The Athenians also considered themselves, with equal justification, to have been descended from the Ionians, who originated in the northern Peloponnese, prior to their migration to Asia Minor, about 1000 BC.[19] In spite of the intriguing speculation of Ramsay and others about the etymological connection between Javan of *Genesis* and the Greek Ion, the consensus today seems to be that the mythical figure of Prometheus also had a prolific human counterpart who had a son named Deucalion, who in turn had a son named Hellen, whose offspring began the civilisation that was to bear his name. His sons Dorus, Aeolus and Xuthus, who was the father of Ion, were the ancestors of the Dorians, Aolians and Ionians. Ion is mentioned by Herodotus, Philochorus, Strabo and Pausanias, as well as Aristotle in his *Metaphysics*, as the patriarch of the Ionians in the Peloponnese, who have been more emphatically described as having been 'Pelasgic and aboriginal in Attica'.[20]

For Pericles, then, as Christine Havelock has noted, 'the promotion of Ionian culture had a political motive: it allowed Athens, a city on the predominantly Doric mainland, to hold up the imperialist banner of pan-Hellenism. The Acropolis buildings, in short, symbolise the supremacy of Greek culture and Greek power in the widest sense'.[21] With this political agenda in mind, which was physically carried through the blending of orders and the immortalisation of the Panathenaia within the frieze of the Parthenon itself, it may be iconoclastic, but certainly not far-fetched to propose that the layering of these imperial associations over the ritualistic functions that were usually associated with a temple in Classical Greece makes the Acropolis an architectural prophet of the Hellenistic Age that was to follow a century and a half later. In their perfection, the buildings on the Acropolis carry the seeds of what critics have categorised as the imperfect age to come. While similar political motives emerge most strongly in the great Altar of Zeus at Pergamon, which was built between 180 and 160 BC and again uses sculptural friezes to symbolise supremacy, or in the Nereid monument at Xanthos, where they describe more sinister intentions, strict typological parallels suggest that the Apollo Temple at Didyma be considered as the Hellenistic equivalent of the Parthenon. In the century and a half that separates the two buildings, quite dramatic changes have obviously taken place. Where the Parthenon has a relatively modest stylobate, the temples of Apollo and the symbolic forest of columns that surround it, are raised up high on seven steps creating a condition that invites entry rather than simply providing a plinth for a piece of sculpture. The habitation of the god itself is reduced to a smaller volume standing in its own idyllic grove within the man-made landscape of columnar trees and cliff-like walls that surround it. This significant change in the perception of the space inside the temple, as a positive, rather than a negative element is once again traceable to beginnings in the design of the cella of the Parthenon, and indicates the major shift in the individual perception of the world that took place in the Hellenistic Age.[22] Alberto Perez Gomez has described this change in world views by saying that:

> The rational explanation of Parmenides and Thales of Miletus brought about the first possibility of dividing human reality into 'subject' and 'object'. As a result, the act of building could later be explained through a logical discourse. This established the possibility for a

theory of architecture such as that of Vitruvius, reinforced with the discovery of the science of geometry, properly speaking, by Euclid. Human action could then be explained through the intellect. A distance was established between design and building. Building, which was originally and primordially a religious, mytho-poetic act, became strictly a rational one, a function of Platonic techne.[23]

While the violations of the Classical canon that accompanied this shift have tended to make this period seem apocryphal to fundamentalists who look upon the Parthenon as a paragon, it is this emphasis on space that also makes Hellenistic architecture seem more comprehensible, and more human, to us today. The realisation that this change began at the Acropolis extends this comprehension back to the Classical model, as well, giving it more than an abstract, iconographic meaning. The introduction of the stoa, which is thought to have been developed in Asia Minor, extended this idea of space to the exterior of building groups as well. While Classical Greek plans, from those of sanctuary compounds to cities in general, consistently show an awareness of the invisible impact that adjacent buildings have upon each other as well as upon those who are moving past them, the stoa had a synergistic effect on this awareness by framing the landscapes and buildings seen through its trabeation, interlocking the space between them.[24] The temple became but one of many major structures linked together in the fabric of the more unified architecture that characterised increasingly integrated civic spaces, where all institutions were promoted equally, making them a combined part of the idea of city itself. Such identification was critical during an age in which the city did not have the time to grow by accretion, but was used instead as both an educational and political vehicle with which to proselytise and colonise new or recalcitrant territories. For this reason the Hippodamian plan, which was even imposed upon topography as forbidding as that at Priene, not only became expedient but necessary, given the shift from the idea of city as polis to that of a frontier post in alien territory. Where religion had managed to remain aloof from politics in the Classical Age, the temple, along with the bouleuterion, gymnasium, theatre, and all other institutions, were seen by Alexander and his successors as the requisite manifestation of Greek culture.

In spite of Alexander's highly dramatised claims of restoring democracy to Asia Minor, and the renewed repetition of this pledge by both he and his successors, politics in its original form effectively disappeared after his invasion, and became the prerogative of the monarch of the moment, as well as the bureaucracy that surrounded him. As R I Winton has said: 'Politics had died, there was no legacy of the city-state as a political organism in the Greek world after Alexander'.[25] Having been crushed at the beginning of the fifth century, the cities of the Ionian League, especially Miletus, who had begun an unsuccessful revolt against the Persians at that time, were particularly susceptible to the forced political inactivity demanded by the Successors, and the buildings that housed governmental activities there were largely for show.[26] This lack of freedom created the curious dichotomy of civic introspection within planned communities at a time of widely expanded geographical horizons.

The polis was not destroyed by the power struggle over Alexander's empire alone, because over-population and the poverty that it was causing on the Greek mainland just prior to the crusade into Asia Minor would eventually have eliminated the city-state on its own. In his *Politics*, Aristotle defined the *koinonia* or community, as an entity that depended upon having enough people in it to make

Herakleia, site plan

it self-sufficient, but not so many that people did not know each other by name.[27] While the polis was not an egalitarian grouping, each person within it had a sense of purpose, and a balance was achieved based on a communal sense of identity. In the larger planned communities of Asia Minor, which were constantly subject to invasion and changing rule, the role of the individual, regardless of station, was irrevocably altered. Alexander as the catalyst for an ideal model of his time, had also helped to bring about this change, in a more personal way, by becoming the self-proclaimed champion of Homeric ideals, and insisting upon becoming a new Achilles. *Agon*, or the competitive spirit that drove Homeric heroes to be the best in any endeavour, was the most important of these ideals, and Alexander's promotion of this attitude through gymnastic games and dramas also tended to eliminate the co-operative spirit that had previously been crucial to the polis, changing the individual's willingness to work with others.

Constant struggle over boundaries and repetitive civic destruction and human suffering were admittedly endemic in Greece prior to the Hellenistic Age but under the Successors this kind of upheaval escalated to new levels. Such uncertainty raised doubts about the efficacy of the traditional supernatural pantheon, and promised interest in foreign cults, such as those of Artemis and Isis, as well as the philosophies of Epicurianism and Stoicism, which all provided escape from the expanding vicissitudes of an increasingly unpredictable and brutal world. By stressing personal, rather than communal needs, each of these cults compounded the idea of individuality, and were reflected in an architecture that catered to a single, rather than collective perspective. From the spaces designed for the living, to the grandiose mausoleum built for the dead, that perspective had more than superficial ramifications, resulting in an architecture that had an interior as well as exterior magnitude. A glance at the plan of the city of Pergamon, for example, indicates a response to more than topographical imperatives, showing an awareness of this primarily individual viewpoint. The result is a centrifugal combination of open forms, rather than a centripetal aggregation of closed spaces, which allowed each person in the city quite literally to appreciate the new horizons that had been opened up to them.[27] While the industrial experience and the subsequent condition of modernity that had been explained so graphically by contemporary writers like Marshall Berman places a nearly impassable barrier between us and a complete understanding of the Hellenistic Age, this surprising dichotomy between a progressive isolation of the individual on the one hand, and the rapid expansion of physical and intellectual horizons on the other is one that we can readily identify with today. While the Greeks of the Classical period may have established the political, philosophical and moral constructs that have eventually come to form the basis of Western civilisation as we know it, the clear cut distinctions of that tradition are no longer operative; and have been replaced by a disillusionment and scepticism that is reminiscent of the Hellenistic Age. The similar questioning of traditional values that we see today, and the introduction of alien ideas into what were once insular, highly conservative societies, give the architectural legacy of this period an added degree of relevance for us today.

NOTES

Introduction

1 Christine Mitchell Havelock, *Hellenistic Art: The Art of the Classical World from the Death of Alexander the Great to the Battle of Actium*, WW Norton & Co, New York, 1981, p 66.

2 Nikos Kazantzakis, *Report to Greco*, Faber and Faber, London, 1973, p 170.

3 *Ibid*, p 136.

4 Ekrem Akurgal, *Ancient Civilisations and Ruins of Turkey*, Haset Kitabevi, Istanbul, 1985, p 267.

5 Havelock, *Hellenistic Art*, *op cit*, p 67.

6 *Ibid*, p 67.

Chapter I – Alexander

1 Homer, *The Iliad*, translated by Robert Fitzgerald, Anchor Books, Doubleday, New York, 1975, p 442.

2 Robin Lane Fox, *The Search for Alexander*, Little Brown and Co, Boston, 1980, p 52.

3 AP Daskalakis, *Alexander the Great and Hellenism*, The Institute for Balkan Studies, Athens, 1966, p 29.

4 Lane Fox, *The Search for Alexander*, *op cit*, pp 61, 82, 84.

5 Daskalakis, *Alexander the Great and Hellenism*, *op cit*, p 16.

6 *Ibid*, p 14.

7 Robin Lane Fox, *Alexander the Great*, Penguin, London, 1988, p 45.

8 WW Tarn, *Alexander the Great*, Beacon Press, Boston, 1956, p 1.

9 Daskalakis, *Alexander the Great and Hellenism*, *op cit*, p 8.

10 *Ibid*, p 36.

11 WW Tarn, *Alexander the Great*, *op cit*, p 8.

12 Homer, *The Iliad*, translated by Robert Fitzgerald, Anchor Books, Doubleday, New York, 1975, p 519.

13 *Ibid*, p 451.

14 *Ibid*, p 454.

15 PR Hardie, 'The Shield of Achilles', *The Journal of Hellenic Studies*, Volume CV, 1985, p 15.

16 *Ibid*, p 25.

17 GMA Hanfmann, *From Croesus to Constantine*, University of Michigan Press, Ann Arbor, Michigan, 1975, p 53.

18 *Ibid*, p 55.

19 Lane Fox, *Alexander the Great*, *op cit*, p 73.

20 Ernest Barker, *The Politics of Aristotle*, Oxford University Press, 1958, p 3.

Chapter II – The Successors

1 WW Tarn, *Hellenistic Civilisation*, Edward Arnold Publishers, London, 1959, pp 6-15.

2 Tarn, *Hellenistic Civilisation*, *op cit*, p 195.

3 Michael Avi-Yonah, *Hellenism and the East*, The Institute of Languages, Literature and the Arts, The Hebrew University, Jerusalem and University Microfilms International, Ann Arbor, Michigan, 1978, p 196.

4 AHM Jones, *The Greek City from Alexander to Justinian*, Clarendon Press, Oxford, 1984, p 19.

5 Avi-Yonah, *Hellenism and the East*, *op cit*, p 207.

6 *Ibid*, p 203.

7 Tarn, *Hellenistic Civilisation*, *op cit*, p 129.

8 *Ibid*, p 128.

9 *Ibid*, pp 127-28.

10 Jones, *The Greek City*, *op cit*, p 7.

11 Avi-Yonah, *Hellenism and the East*, *op cit*, p 219.

12 Jones, *The Greek City*, *op cit*, p 22.

13 Edmund Bacon, *The Design of Cities*, Viking, New York, 1963. This book contains an entire chapter on the evolution of the Athenian Agora and Acropolis.

14 Constantine Doxiades, *Architectural Space in Ancient Greece*, MIT Press, Cambridge, Massachusetts, 1972.

Chapter III – The Cities

1 Michael Grant, *The Rise of the Greeks*, Charles Scribner & Sons, New York, 1988, pp 2 and 137.

2 *Genesis*, 10: 1-4, *Holy Bible*, New International Version, Zondervan, New Jersey, 1978, p 6.

3 Sir William Ramsay, *Asiatic Elements in Greek Civilisation*, The Gifford Lectures in the University of Edinburgh 1915-16, London, 1927, p 243.

4 Grant, *The Rise of the Greeks*, *op cit*, p 140.

5 Ramsay, *Asiatic Elements*, *op cit*, p 140.

6 Grant, *The Rise of the Greeks*, *op cit*, p 17.

7 *Ibid*, p 290.

8 Ramsay, *Asiatic Elements*, *op cit*, p 5.

9 Grant, *The Rise of the Greeks*, *op cit*, p 5.

10 Vincent Scully, *The Earth, the Temple, and the Gods*, Yale University Press, New Haven and London, 1969.

11 Akurgal, *Ancient Civilisations and Ruins of Turkey*, *op cit*, p 210.

12 Many sources differ on the exact time of this collaboration, with several authorities placing it in the reign of Xerxes, and his return through Asia Minor after the Persian defeat at Plataea in 479 BC. See, George EE Bean, *Aegean Turkey*, Ernest Benn, London and WW Norton, New York, 1966, p 195, as well as HW Parke, 'The Massacre of the Branchidae', *The Journal of Hellenic Studies*, Volume CV, 198, pp 59 to 68. The weight of their evidence seems to favour Darius.

13 See Parke, 'The Massacre of the Branchidae', *op cit*, p 68.

14 Grant, *The Rise of the Greeks*, *op cit*, p 164.

15 Hanfmann, *From Croesus to Constantine*, *op cit*.

16 *Ibid*, p 22. See, also, GMA Richter, *Sculpture and Sculptors of the Greeks*, Yale University Press, New Haven, 1970, pp 174-5.

17 Hanfmann, *From Croesus to Constantine*, *op cit*.

18 *Acts* 23-25, *Holy Bible*, *op cit*, p 675.

19 See Michael Wood, *In Search of the Trojan War*, BBC,

London, 1985, p 43.

20 Akurgal, *Ancient Civilisations and Ruins of Turkey*, *op cit*, p 240.

21 For a comprehensive tally, see Grant, *The Rise of the Greeks*, *op cit*, pp 65 and 137-8.

22 Hanfmann, *From Croesus to Constantine*, *op cit*, p 5. Dr Hanfmann has been the director of archaeological excavations at Sardis (Sart) since 1958.

23 *Ibid*, p 7.

24 Michael Avi-Yonah, *Hellenism and the East*, *op cit*, p 128.

26 See Scully, *The Earth, the Temple, and the Gods*, *op cit*.

Chapter IV – The Institutions

1 Tarn, *Hellenistic Civilisation*, *op cit*, p 134.

2 *Ibid*, p 135.

3 *Ibid*, p 140.

4 See, Akurgal, *Ancient Civilisations and Ruins of Turkey*, *op cit*, pp 147-154.

5 *Ibid*, pp 226-231.

6 Scully, *The Earth, the Temple and the Gods*, *op cit*, p 171.

7 *Ibid*. The thesis is eloquently expressed throughout Scully's book.

8 See Bacon, *The Design of Cities*, *op cit*. The author makes this point very effectively in his entire chapter on the evolution of Athens.

9 VA Tobin, *'MAAT and DIKE; Some Comparative Considerations of Egyptian and Greek Thought'*, *Journal of the American Research Centre in Egypt*, Vol XXIV, 1986, pp 113-121.

10 Michael Avi-Yonah, *Hellenism and the East*, *op cit*, p 38.

11 *Ibid*, p 40.

12 *Ibid*, p 39.

13 *Ibid*, p 29.

14 *Ibid*, pp 34-36.

15 Walter Burkett, *Homo Necans*, University of California Press, Berkeley, and Los Angeles, California, 1983, p 11, note 46.

16 Wolfgang Radt, *Pergamon: An Archaeological Guide*, Touring Club of Turkey, Istanbul, 1984, p 12.

17 Burkett, *Homo Necans*, *op cit*, p 11.

18 *Ibid*, p 2.

19 *Ibid*, p 5. See also the excellent sources noted by Burkett, especially S Dow and DH Gill, *'The Greek Cult Table'*, *American Journal of Archaeology* 69, 1965, pp 103-114, and E Kadletz, *Animal Sacrifice in Greek and Roman Religion*, doctoral dissertation, University of Washington, 1976.

20 *Ibid*, p 23.

Chapter V – The Hellenistic Legacy

1 MI Finley, (ed) *The Legacy of Greece*, Clarendon Press, Oxford, 1981, p 2.

2 David Theodore Fyfe, *Hellenistic Architecture: An Introductory Study*, Cambridge University Press, 1936, p 3.

3 JMC Toynbee, *The Art of the Romans*, Thames and Hudson,

London, 1965, p 16. Toynbee here is delightfully frank about Roman capabilities in this area, saying that they 'were not, it seems, naturally endowed with creative artistic genius'. (p 15).

4 Axel Boethus, *Etruscan and Early Roman Architecture*, Penguin, London, 1978, p 106.

5 Toynbee, *The Art of the Romans*, *op cit*, p 16.

6 *Ibid*, p 20.

7 Boethus, *Etruscan and Early Roman Architecture*, *op cit*, p 137; (quoting Livy XXXIX 6-7).

8 *Ibid*, pp 136-7.

9 *Ibid*, p 176.

10 LB Moss, *Birth of the Middle Ages*, Oxford University Press, 1935, p 253.

11 James Steele, *Turkey, A Traveller's Historical and Architectural Guide*, Scorpion, London, l990, pp 11-13.

12 See, for example, De Lubicz, RA Schwaller, *Le Temple de l'Homme*, Vol II, pp 322-49, for Babylonian and Egyptian mathematics.

13 AH Armstrong, in HJ Jones, *The Greeks*, AC Watts Co, London, 1962, p 62.

14 MI Rostovtsev, *The Social and Economic History of the Hellenistic World*, Vol 3, Oxford University Press, 1941, p 1234.

15 Robert Adam, *Ruins of the Palace of the Emperor Diocletian at Spalato in Dalmatia*, London, 1764.

16 Fyfe, *op cit*, p 72: 'From their resemblances to work in Asia Minor and Syria, it would not be out of place to call the detailed treatment of Spalato Hellenistic'.

17 Havelock, *Hellenistic Art*, *op cit*, p 66.

18 AH Armstrong, in HJ Jones, *The Greeks*, *op cit*, p 391.

19 JM Cook, *The Greeks in Ionia and the East*, Thames and Hudson, London, 1962, p 21.

20 G Clinton, *Fasti Hellenici*, Oxford University Press, 1834, p 11.

21 Havelock, *Hellenistic Art*, *op cit*, p 66.

22 *Ibid*, p 67.

23 Alberto Perez Gomez, *The City as a Paradigm of Symbolic Order*, The Carlton Book, Carlton University School of Architecture, Ottawa, Canada, 1986, p 7.

24 Bacon, *The Design of Cities*, *op cit*, p 55. For an exhaustive study of the geometric relationships between Classical buildings, see: Doxiades, *Architectural Space in Ancient Greece*, *op cit*, 1972.

25 Finley (ed), *The Legacy of Greece*, *op cit*; RI Winton, *'Political Theory'*, p 34.

26 *Ibid*, p 392.

27 *Ibid*, p 11.

28 Havelock, *Hellenistic Art*, *op cit*, p 115. These terms are used in relationship to Hellenistic sculpture, but are equally appropriate here.

Neandria

Neandria is located inland from Alexandria Troas, and originally occupied a one thousand, four hundred-metre-long, four hundred and fifty-metre-wide strip of fortified hilltop near Mount Çigri. The polygonal walls, which date from the fifth century BC, were nearly three-metres wide in some places which accounts for their survival. Early excavations by Robert Koldewey in 1899 uncovered a temple with a row of seven columns running down the middle of the cella to support the roof gable above. Most important of all, however, was his discovery of archaic, voluted capitals that have since been shown, by PP Bentancourt in The Aeolic Style in Architecture, to have been the basis for the Ionic order.

Assos

Distinctly divided into acropolis, civic agora and port as it marches down its steep hillside, Assos occupies a site of incomparable beauty, and its structures are now much diminished. The Hellenistic walls around the acropolis, however, as well as fragments of the circuit wall, still remain, because of their massiveness, with the majority of the remainder having been used to build the village of Behramkale, nearby. Many of the speculative re-creations of the fan-shaped agora typically give the impression of a flat site, whereas the difference in elevation between it and the agora is actually quite dramatic. This change in level was used to great advantage by the builders of the agora, who used a multi-levelled stoa at the base of the cliff as both a retaining wall and a raised colonnaded street, linking the square bouleuterion at its narrow end, with a small temple precinct, opposite. The exquisitely carved marble quay that once created a safe harbour in the lower port, is still intact and visible below the surface of the water, looking much as it did when Aristotle taught here.

OPPOSITE: Hellenistic watchtower along the wall of the acropolis.

ABOVE: The Temple of Athena at Assos is an anomaly since it was built in the Doric order, in spite of the fact that it is in the middle of Ionia.

Pergamon

As one of the most influential cities of the Hellenistic Age, Pergamon also represents its most cherished ideals. A sense of autonomy and the pre-eminence of the intellect guided the ordering of its plan which clings to a steep mountainside and revolves around the theatre in its centre. The palaces of the Attalids, rather than the temples, occupy the high ground and the remains of the Red Hall, more accurately named the Temple of Serapis, tower over the contemporary city, as a reminder of the diffusion of religious influence at this time. The city was ceded to the Romans by Attalus III.

In direct contrast to the dramatically sloping site of Pergamon, the Asklepeion is situated in a flat, wooded glade, sheltered by low hills to the north. It is linked to the city by a sacred way, the Via Tecta, which joins its propylon at an acute angle, resolving the difference between the adaptation of the complex to its specific site with the most expeditious footpath from its mother city. Various structures of incredible variety are attached to a rectangular enclosure wall, which protects a spring in its centre that was considered to have the capacity to heal those who drank from it. Galen, practised and taught here, compiling empirical treatises that were consulted until the Middle Ages. The emphasis of treatment was on spiritual and psychological well being as a pre-requisite for physical health.

OPPOSITE: The north colonnade of the Asklepeion.

OVERLEAF: View of the Asklepeion towards the theatre, to the north through the south stoa.

p 80: Part of the south stoa of the Asklepeion.

p 81 ABOVE LEFT AND RIGHT: In direct contravention of the popular misconception that the Greeks did not know how to build an arch, the water system at Pergamon is built exclusively with this structural system which was considered to be appropriate for utilitarian purposes; BELOW LEFT: The site of the Great Altar of Zeus, which has since been removed to the Berlin Museum. The Altar is a remarkable example of the use of ornamental sculpture in architecture, meant in this case to appease the Gauls, who were constantly threatening Pergamon; BELOW RIGHT: The north colonnade of the Asklepeion inner precinct, in the Ionian order.

pp 82-83: The Via Tecta, which linked the Asklepeion with the city of Pergamon.

p 84: The Temple of Serapis was given the vernacular name of the 'Kizul Avlu' or Red Hall because of its deep crimson colour, but is now known to have been a temple dedicated to Serapis, the God of the Underworld. Its location seems incongruous to those without some knowledge of the relationship that existed between the city of Pergamon on the mountain top to the north-east of the 'Hall' and the Asklepeion to the south-west; the building is almost equi-distant between the two with a central position on the Via Tecta. Large fragments of statues executed in the Egyptian style that have been found buried here show the extent of the influence of foreign, and particularly Egyptian deities at this time. The peculiar position of the temple is also significant because it was intended to straddle the river Selinus, which is now called the Uçkemer Cayi, because of ablution pools in its lower storey. Two tower-like structures that flanked the main entrance were reserved for this ritual, which has not been normally associated with traditional Classical Greek practice. A set of huge, vaulted tunnels located beneath the temples made a direct connection with the river possible, showing that some kind of ritualistic water immersion was obviously an integral part of the building's function.

p 85: The Temple of Dionysus on the lower terrace of the Pergamon hillside, representing one of the best examples of Hellenistic frontality in temple design.

Sardis

Croesus was the fifth and most famous ruler after Gyges to govern Sardis prior to its capture by the Persians in 546 BC. It then became the western terminus of the Royal Road which began at Susa, making it an especially symbolic destination for Alexander, who took it in 334 BC. It subsequently came under Seleucid, and finally Pergamene influence before being ceded to the Romans. The gold-bearing Pactolus river was the source of Croesus' fabled wealth, which also made the city one of the most influential in Asia Minor.

OPPOSITE: Facade of the theatre, Sardis, built in the Hellenistic period and expanded by the Romans.

ABOVE AND BELOW: The marble court, Sardis.

OVERLEAF: Forecourt of the synagogue at Sardis (third century AD).

pp 90-91: Fountain in the synagogue atrium.

pp 92-93: Originally built in 300 BC, the Temple of Artemis replaced an archaic altar that had existed here. The final phase of construction was completed in 150 AD.

Ephesus

As the traditional enclosure of the Anatolian goddess Cybele, Ephesus had strong religious affiliations prior to Greek colonisation when this cult was converted to that of Artemis. Lysimachus expanded the area of the city to extend between Mount Koressos and Mount Pion inside a nine-kilometre-long perimeter wall. After 190 BC, the city came under the rule of the Pergamene kings, and was ceded to the Romans with the rest of his kingdom by Attalus III.

OPPOSITE: The Herakles gate, built by the Romans in the early fifth century at the south-eastern end of Curetes Street.

ABOVE: Sculptural frieze.

OVERLEAF: Carved into a mountainside in typical Greek fashion, the theatre was originally built in the Hellenistic period and then more rows were added by Claudius, Nero and Trajan. The Hellenistic skene has been encorporated into the Roman stage. It lies at the end of the Arcadiane, also constructed in Hellenistic times and embellished by the Emperor Arcadius.

p 98: The Herakles gateway.

pp 99 ABOVE AND BELOW: The theatre at Ephesus.

p 100: The Temple of Hadrian. Many of the best preserved structures in Ephesus, such as this small temple, are Roman. The arch here is of particular interest, since it indicates a change in the Greek attitude towards trabeation in religious structures. An exquisite head of Tyche, or Fortune, whose popularity began to rise late in the Hellenistic Age because of the chaos of the time, is used as a keystone.

p 101: Curates Street.

pp 102-103: The Library of Celsus, built in 110 AD, shows an extension of the Hellenistic inventiveness with facades, using a theatrical prototype for its highly visible, eastern elevation.

Magnesia on the Maeander

Column capital from the Temple of Artemis, built between 150 and 125 BC, attributed by Vitruvius to the influential Hellenistic architect Hermogenes, front and side views. As the traditional home of a people called the Magnetes, this city may also have been named by colonists from Magnesia, in Thessaly, who came into the area in 650 BC. The temple from which this capital survives, was one of the largest in Asia Minor, with a famous Amazon frieze that has now been parcelled out among several museums.

Priene

Because of the steepness of its site, few cities of the Hellenistic period can compare to Priene as an example of the adaptability of the Hippodamian grid. In spite of the consistent use of the right angle in its layout, there is a great deal of variety and hierarchy in the civic spaces that are created, and a notable lack of repetition. This hierarchy extends from the open public areas, such as the agora to the private houses, which were typically organised around a central court. The agora here was a long, rectangular space in the middle of the city that had a stoa running along the entire length of the uphill side with a square terrace facing it. While the streets were steeply inclined, these flat courts were retained by the foundation walls of the buildings that surrounded them, providing a balanced, horizontal counterpoint that is similar to that found in Greek villages such as the Hora on the island of Patmos today. The institutions within the city, such as the Temple of Athena, the theatre and the gymnasium all branch off from the streets that traverse the slope, becoming sporadic, and well-positioned episodes along the path. Like Herakleia, Miletus, Patara and Knidos, Priene has long since lost its harbour, known as Naulochos, to the sedimentation of the centuries.

OPPOSITE: Located at the highest point in the city, the Temple of Athena was built in the middle of the fourth century BC by Pytheos, who also built the Mausoleum of Halicarnassos. It is a good example of the refinement of the Ionic order in Asia Minor.
ABOVE: The steep cliff behind Priene.

Miletus

In its original topographical configuration, as a long peninsula with four harbours carved into it, Miletus was ideally suited to its role as the premier city of Ionia, and the starting point for colonial expansions into the Mediterranean, Black Sea and Egypt. Its leadership of the Ionian revolt against the Persians in 494 BC, however, ended its autonomy, and by the time Alexander arrived in Asia Minor, it had just begun to recover a portion of its past glory. It is perhaps most famous for the scientists, philosophers and geometers it has produced, such as Thales, Anaximenes, Hekataios and Anaximander, as well as Hippodamos, who was responsible for its gridiron plan. The harbours have since silted up, leaving the city in the middle of a plain.

OPPOSITE: Roman statue of Zeus in front of nymphaeum, 79-80 AD.

ABOVE: The Theatre of Miletus was built in four phases during the Hellenistic period and held about five thousand people. Clear masonry divisions differentiate the Hellenistic and Roman parts of the structure, which were added later, increasing its capacity to fifteen thousand. The front columns of the shading baldachin over the seat of honour, occupied by the Roman emperor during visits to the city, can still be seen.

OVERLEAF: Theatre from the north.

p 112 ABOVE: Steps and columns along the south agora; BELOW: View of the theatre showing a scroll bracket and Ionic capital.

p 113 ABOVE: Doric colonnade with sculptured marble detail; BELOW: West agora, near the stadium.

pp 114-115: The Delphinion, which marks a spot felt to be sacred to Apollo Delphinios, was erected in the Hellenistic period. Dolphins were associated with the god because of their intelligence and response to music, and small statues of them once adorned the sides of the tholos. A propylon, as well as an enclosing stoa was added by the Romans. The landlocked island of Lade can be seen in the distance.

Arycanda

Located beside the Arycanda river, fifteen miles north of Finike and Limyra in the Beydag mountains, the ruins of this Lycian city, which was founded in the fifth century BC, are unusual in several aspects. In addition to incrementally stepping up the mountainside, which provides breathtaking distant views from each of its public spaces, the agora in the centre terrace is situated in a lower, excavated space, surrounded by a raised colonnaded market above it.

Labranda

As with Termessos, isolation has helped to ensure the preservation of one of the most remote archaeological sites in Asia Minor, which was connected to Mylasa with a sacred way. A prostyle temple, dedicated to Zeus, as well as the sacred precinct around it, are thought to have been realised by Mausolos between 377 and 353 BC. The foundation wall of the east terrace indicates the ingenuity used in fitting the sacred precinct into a steeply sloping, and heavily wooded site; beneath a cliff face rising abruptly to the north above the Temple of Zeus.

Hierapolis

Founded by Pergamon, Hierapolis prospered as a Roman city between the second and third centuries AD, as these Roman baths testify. Now known as Pamukkale, it lies between Caria, Phrygia and Lydia, on a long, narrow plateau of white limestone. King Eumenes II established the city in 190 BC, as a military colony, to retain territory, and it is believed to be named after Hiera, the wife of Telephos, who figures prominently in the foundation myth of Pergamon. A theatre, to the north of the city, is all that remains of the Hellenistic community, with the majority of buildings having been destroyed by earthquakes.

Aphrodisias

Located in the Maeander Valley, in the district of Caria, this city was also known as Ninoe, suggesting the strong affiliation between the Akkadian goddess Nin and the goddess Aphrodite in the area of Asia Minor. Further similarities also exist between the attributes ascribed to this goddess and Cybele or Artemis, who were also felt to be connected with nature and fertility. A marble quarry near the city supported the inauguration of the 'School of Aphrodisias', and many highly original sculptures, as well as copies, were produced here. An extensive circuit wall, which still survives in places, once enclosed the enormous confines of the city, which shows evidence of having been established as early as 2500 BC. The Temple of Aphrodite is the main structure still standing on the site, and was erected in the later part of the Hellenistic Age. Recent excavations by Professor Kenan Erim, conducted under the auspices of New York University, indicate that the Hellenistic temple was octostyle, with a temenos added by the Emperor Hadrian, sometime between 117 and 138 AD, which also served as a school of philosophy.

pp 138-142: Temple of Aphrodite, first century BC.

p 143: Part of the postern gate, near the city wall.

Herakleia under Latmos

Like Miletus and Troy, this city was once near the sea, and was called Latmos, in connection with the mountain that rises above it. An extensive city wall was built by Alexander's general, Lysimachus, in 287 BC, to encompass a Hippodamian grid. The Hellenistic agora is the central focus of the plan.

OPPOSITE: The Temple of Athena, on a promontory overlooking the city.

ABOVE AND BELOW: The walls of Herakleia.

OVERLEAF: The Sanctuary of Endymion, the shepherd, whom the moon goddess Selene visited nightly on Mount Latmos.

Knidos

As a member of the Dorian Hexopolis which also included Kos, Lindos, Salysos, Kamiros and Halicarnassos, the city of Knidos, grew rich as a commercial port. It is best known as the birthplace of the mathematician Eudoxos, and the architect Sostratos, who designed the lighthouse of Alexandria.

ABOVE: The theatre, looking south-east.

BELOW: The theatre, with the lighthouse in the distance that marks the entrance to the ancient harbour.

Kekova

Located next to Aperlae in ancient Lycia, Kekova is now located on a small offshore island. Because of the rising water level, this rocky outcropping is all that remains of the ancient town of Teimiussa. The remains of tombs and houses can still be seen beneath the clear blue water surrounding the island, with many sarcophaghi seeming to float along the surface.

Xanthos

A mysterious aura surrounds Xanthos, which was the head of the Lycian League, and renowned for its fierce independence. The site, which is situated on a high bluff above the Xanthos river consists of the ancient Lycian acropolis at its western promontory, and the later, Roman acropolis on higher ground to the north. Charles Fellows was the first to bring the ruins to the attention of the West in 1838, and was responsible for the removal of the reliefs on the Harpy Tomb as well as the entire Nereid Monument to the British Museum soon afterwards.

OPPOSITE AND ABOVE: A pair of sarcophagi surmounting the back wall of the theatre, consisting of a pillar tomb on the right, and the Harpy tomb on the left. Nearly nine-metres high, the Harpy tomb which dates from the first part of the fifth century, was named after the reliefs of winged figures carrying off representations of the dead carved on its upper funerary chamber. The style of the carvings indicates a date somewhere between 480 and 470 BC.

BELOW: Built just outside the north wall of the ancient Lycian acropolis near the Xanthos river, this theatre has remained relatively intact because it was built in the Roman period. It has replaced its Hellenistic counterpart, which remains buried nearby.

Patara

Beyond the man-made rock ledges of the theatre, with its backdrop of open green fields, was one of the busiest harbours in Lycia, marked by a lighthouse that once stood on a hill in the background. The main part of the city, including a temple to an unidentified deity, lies directly above the theatre. The top of the slope, into which it is built, gives an unobstructed, panoramic view towards the Mediterranean. Many of the ruins that remain are Roman, rather than Hellenistic in date, indicating that the city may have reached its peak of prosperity at that time; Hannibal, Hadrian and St Paul are known to have stopped at Patara's port.

As one of the most centrally located of a group of cities that also included Myra, Tlos, Pinara, Olympos and Xanthos, Patara was the logical meeting place for the Lycian League. A deep well at the top of the hill above the theatre may have been the source of water for both the acropolis and a residential district that was located on a peninsula projecting out into the harbour below. As with many of the Hellenistic cities in Asia Minor, Patara has yet to be fully excavated, and so many of the questions raised by its partially visible remains have yet to be answered. They are left lying buried beneath the sand that has now covered the city.

OPPOSITE: Gateway dating from about 100 AD, behind a Lycian sarcophagus.

ABOVE: The granary, built during the reign of Hadrian.

OVERLEAF: Looking out over a plain that was once the ancient harbour of Patara, the theatre was extended to its present form in the second century AD.

pp 164-165: The view to the west from the theatre.

Sidyma

In his book, Discoveries in Lycia, Charles Fellows documented several characteristic types of tombs that he found there, with accompanying drawings. Those at Sidyma differ from the 'horse's mane' profile found at Xanthos, in that they are pedimented, with stylised acroterai, which give them a temple-like appearance, as opposed to the visual connections with a domestic prototype used elsewhere. The hard grey rock found in this region gives a uniformity to the architecture as seen in the few public buildings and gateways that still exist.

Myra

Rock cut tombs in the cliff face near Myra, dating from the fourth century BC. The cliffs rise abruptly from the Demre Dere river, which was the Myros, and the coastal plain in front of it. There was once an important Lycian city here, which is difficult to surmise given the size of the small town of Kale, or Demre that has replaced it. The tombs have been built over a span of many centuries, with some of them dating back to the fourth century BC. Many different Lycian prototypes are represented here.
pp 176-177: Roman theatre, Myra.

Perge

Except for the acropolis which terminates the major axis that runs through the middle of Perge, the site of the city is flat. The crumbling remains of the round stone towers that formed the framework for the second, inner gateway dramatically punctuate this flatness, and it is easy to imagine the large triangular space between the first and second gate being full of people travelling in and out of the city. Merchants' temporary wooden stalls were built against the stone walls here to take full advantage of all the activity. The raucous, colourful spectacle that resulted must have been a daily source of amusement to the guards stationed on the ramparts above. As in other Hellenistic cities in the Near East, such as Jerash, such shops would have undoubtedly continued along both sides of the main spine; once inside the gates merchants would have been accommodated within flanking colonnades. Shop-lined streets such as this, which may have developed as a consequence of the increase in cosmopolitan trade during this period, were further developed by the Romans, and were distinctly different from those grouped around the Classical Greek agora. The culmination of this linear arrangement at Perge was a high, irregularly shaped acropolis which was later refined by the addition of a semi-circular nymphaeum. A second major street, which ran in an east-west direction across the cardo maximus, also had gates at each end and led to a palaestra built during the reign of the Emperor Claudius, between 41 and 54 AD.

OPPOSITE: Detail of Ionic capital and architrave.

p 180: Sculptured panel in the theatre precinct.

Sillyon

Because of its isolation at the top of a high rock outcropping, Sillyon, which is located north of Perge and Aspendos, remains relatively intact, presenting a good example of a complete Hellenistic city. A ramp leads up from a stadium on the lower slope of the hill to the acropolis and main city above, where most of the public buildings, such as the theatre, are located. A high encircling wall closely follows the contour of the mountain ridge.

OPPOSITE: Main gateway through the wall into the acropolis.

ABOVE: View from the wall.

BELOW: Fragments of the city's aqueduct.

p 204: Ramp and stair leading up to the city.

p 205: Statuary fragment at the bottom of the mountain.

Phaselis

Ingeniously sited to span between a wide, arc-shaped harbour and a smaller circular one at the neck of a club-shaped peninsula projecting into the Mediterranean, Phaselis is organised along a central spine that opens up as it approaches the theatre in the centre of the city. The peninsula is heavily wooded, with low, umbrella-shaped pines, which now cover all but its cardo, and the aqueduct that once served it. Alexander lingered here for quite some time before moving east, perhaps because of the beauty of the city.

OPPOSITE AND ABOVE: The aqueduct, which brought water from the mountains, to the north.

p 224: The nymphaeum.

p 225: The eastern harbour.

Termessos

Located in the rugged mountains north of Side and Perge, Termessos was by-passed by Alexander during his eastward march through Asia Minor because of the great difficulty that would have been involved in an assault. Sheer cliffs behind the stage of its theatre are far more dramatic than the contour lines of its site plan convey, allowing a clear view to the mountain looming opposite. Narrow, switchback footpaths provide the only access to the city from the valley below, which it dominated in the past, extracting duty from all who wished to pass. Its population was reputed to be fiercely independent, and tough, and after experiencing the topography of their city, it is easy to see why many of the buildings here, especially the gymnasium directly to the north of the theatre, are in a fine state of preservation.

OPPOSITE: All of the buildings of Termessos were built of the same hard grey stone from the mountain it is located on, giving it a monochromatic appearance that joins it to its site.

ABOVE: Detail of a coffered ceiling, showing chimera.

p 228: Detail of a wall with niches.

p 229: The Theatre of Termessos.

pp 230-231: The Theatre of Termessos is so high that it frequently projects above the clouds. Recent restoration has cleared most debris, caused by earthquakes in this region.

p 232: The aqueduct which brought water to the city.

p 233: A monument erected in honour of a visit by the Emperor Hadrian, on the lower slopes of the mountain.

Olba (Diocaesarea)

The city of Diocaesarea was once home to the Teucrids, who were a religiously based dynasty that dominated western Cilicia in the Hellenistic period. Excavated by E Herzfeld in 1907, it is now known as Uzuncaburç, or High Tower, because of a five-storey fortification, dating from about 200 BC, that still stands here.

The Temple of Zeus has thirty columns still intact, but the cella was intentionally destroyed when it was converted into a church.
OPPOSITE: Temple of Zeus, third century BC.
ABOVE: Colonnaded street, Olba, built by the Romans.
pp 236-237: Colonnaded street, details.

Isparta

Sculpted pediment in Isparta, located north of Perge, Aspendos and Sillyon. The use of such realistic anthropomorphic figures as ornament in religious structures, rather than idealised human forms, is typical in Hellenistic architecture, as can also be seen in the mausoleum at Halicarnassos, and the famous Medusa head frieze on the Temple of Apollo at Didyma. This head, however, is even more common, anticipating the severe features of Roman portraiture to follow.

Ankara

The Temple of Augustus and Rome, in Ankara, was built between 25 and 20 BC; shortly after the annexation of the province of Galatia by Rome. It was the prototype for the Temple of Zeus at Aizanoi, and faces west in the tradition of its Hellenistic predecessors. The acanthus leaves of the column capitals, however, are not as well executed as in earlier temples.

Nemrut Dag

The kingdom of Kommagene is an example of the megalomania and cultural interaction that characterised the Hellenistic period, which had its last gasp here. Established by Mithradates I Kallinikos at the end of the Seleucid dynasty, its hegemony expanded under his son, Antiochos I Ephiphanes, between 62-32 BC, until it was ended by the Roman Emperor Vespasian in 72 AD. The tumulus that survives today has terraces on its east and west sides, connected by a processional way, located at the top of Nemrut Dag. Antiochos constructed a genealogy that included Darius I of Persia, through his father and Alexander the Great, through his mother; and expressed this in his hierotheseion.

OPPOSITE: The head of Herakles-Artagnes, following the custom of multiple inscription typically used with deities in the Hellenistic period.

ABOVE AND OVERLEAF: The Hierotheseion of Antiochos I, looking towards the east terrace, first century BC.

p 244: Antiochos I.

p 245: Zeus-Ahuramazda.

Aizanoi

Having been settled in the first century BC, Aizanoi reached the zenith of its power in the second century AD, when the Temple of Zeus, theatre and stadium were built. In spite of its date the temple, which is the best preserved sacred building from this period in Asia Minor, continues the pseudo-arrangement proscribed by Hermogenes as a rule during the late Hellenistic Age, and the high podium base is also indicative of this era.

OPPOSITE: The porch of the Temple of Zeus.
ABOVE: Sculptured fragment of an entablature.
p 248: The Temple of Zeus built between 117 and 138 AD, during the reign of Hadrian.
p 249: View up through the peristasis, in the Temple.
pp 250-251: The theatre, looking south down the length of the stadium that was attached to it.